Algarve

- A ☛ in the text denotes a highly recommended sight
- A complete A–Z of practical information starts on p.102
- Extensive mapping on cover flaps

Berlitz Publishing Company, Inc.

Princeton   Mexico City   Dublin   Eschborn   Singapore

Text: Paul Murphy
Editor: Sarah Hudson
Photography: Paul Murphy, Claude Huber
Layout: Media Content Marketing, Inc.
Cartography: GeoSystems

Thanks to the Portuguese National Tourist Office, Maria Inês Caeiro Martins and TAP Air Portugal for their assistance in the preparation of this guide.

Although the publisher tries to insure the accuracy of all the information in this book, changes are inevitable and errors may result. The publisher cannot be responsible for any resulting loss, inconvenience, or injury. If you find an error in this guide, please let the editors know by writing to Berlitz Publishing Company, 400 Alexander Park, Princeton, NJ 08540-6306.

ISBN 2-8315-6284-8
Revised 1998 – Second Printing June 1999

Printed in Switzerland by Weber SA, Bienne
029/906 RP

CONTENTS

Maps

Algarve

THE PROVINCE AND THE PEOPLE

Portugal's southernmost province has enough sandy beaches to toast every sunbather in Europe. Magical secluded coves and golden strands stretch as far as the eye can see. The ocean may be the Atlantic, but the Algarve has a definite Mediterranean feel.

Gnarled old women, wearing bonnets to keep the sun off their already leather-tanned faces, sit on walls in out-of-the-way villages of squat white houses. Their menfolk, sporting black felt hats, shuffle about their daily business by bicycle or donkey, or simply sit in groups discussing the day's events, curiously eyeing the tourists. Meanwhile, on a beach they share with sunbathers, fishermen repaint their boats in colours nearly as bright as the flowers on the cliffs above. Not all old and new rub shoulders harmoniously, however—karaoke bars are beginning to usurp the old fado houses, high-rise buildings loom over the old-style white houses, and cars cause chaos in small villages that were designed for rather less horsepower.

Ode to the Algarve

The local poet Cândido Guerreiro (1871–1954) summed up the feel of the Algarve thus:

Em fevereiro, quando lá de cima
Deus, com tinta de luar, escreve
Seus lindos versos algarvios, rima
A flor das amendoeiras com a neve...
When in February from heaven
God writes his Algarve poetry in moonlight
His beautiful verses rhyme
The blossoms of the almond trees with snow

The south coast of Portugal—about 160 km (100 miles) of sand catering for all tastes—is neatly divided into the flat, beachy Sotavento to the east, and the rugged Barlavento to the west. The latter boasts the famous ochre cliffs and surreally eroded rock formations that portray a life-and-death struggle between land and sea, and the east is a harmonious marriage of coast and ocean. This intimate co-existence continues inland, sloping up through pines, mimosa, eucalyptus, and heather to an altitude of nearly 915 metres (3,000 feet), with landscapes more akin to northern Europe. These highlands on the southern exposure are a great bonus for holiday-makers wanting to escape the madding crowds.

The Algarve climate is the best in all Portugal, and one of the kindest in the world. The region basks in more than 250 days of sunshine a year, more than almost any other international resort area. No wonder the Algarve is famous

A brightly painted house atop the hillside in Foia.

While travelling on the backroads you'll find little has changed for some Algarve folks over the years.

for unbeatable golf facilities, and that riding and tennis are so popular. The moderating effect of the Gulf Stream manages to maintain a fresh springtime feel throughout the Algarve winter, while in summer the heat rarely becomes unbearable. The most romantic time to come is between late January and February, when a sea of white almond blossom covers the fields.

The Algarve has had a chequered history. It was occupied by the Moors from the eighth to the 13th centuries, then after the Reconquest (see page 16) found itself at the forefront of world exploration. The man leading the team of discoverers who would chart the unknown seas and open up much of the globe for world trade was Prince Henry (Infante Henrique) the Navigator. In fact, a large part of this work was financed by Henry's royalties from the Algarve fishing industry.

A young boy and his dog take a break— typical of the relaxed atmosphere in Algarve.

During the last couple of centuries, however, Portugal has had little to smile about, buffeted by wars and constitutional crises, and the Algarve has remained something of a poor relation to Europe. Its current status as a major tourist destination is a relatively recent phenomenon—the first resort, Praia da Rocha (see page 61), was "discovered" in the 1930s. There have been, however, illustrious visitors from Roman times right through the Middle Ages, and up to the

Edwardian period, when the travellers came to take the waters at the Monchique spa (see page 55).

Sadly, the lessons of the Spanish costas have not been learned (despite protestations to the contrary), and some damage has already been done to much of the coastline. It's not hard to find good beaches on the Algarve, but some of the developments that accompany them do not complement the natural beauty of the land, although a concession to this is that the newer ones are at least of the low-rise variety.

Remarkably, in the face of a certain touristic onslaught, the Algarve still retains much of its old-fashioned charm. Just cross to the north of the main EN 125 route and you are in a different world. The countryside, with its flowering orchards, lush rice paddies, and undulating fields of grain, shows the continuing importance of agriculture in the local economy. The pace of life is slow, and you'll still see the type of rustic vignette that is either dead or dying out elsewhere in Europe.

For centuries, fishing has been intimately linked with life on the Algarve. Wherever you go on the coast you'll be alongside fishermen, either the crews of small boats who work just

All over Algarve you will see delicate, filigreed chimney tops in bright colours.

Fishermen and their boats loaded with goods are a common sight along the Algarve shore.

offshore, or the trawlermen who go far out in search of big shoals and even into distant waters for the *bacalhau* (cod) that are so beloved by the Portuguese. In fishing villages, too, life is simple, unaffected, and continuing much as it has for centuries.

Go along to the local fish market for a further insight into the domestic way of life. The bargaining is serious, but not to the exclusion of wry interplay between seller and buyer. The same scenario is played out a thousand times a day at markets all over the region. Every town has a market day at least once a month, to which farmers bring their livestock to trade; artisans and itinerant vendors sell their wares, not just to tourists but to each other. It would be a shame not to attend at least one market day during your stay.

The easiest way of getting round the Algarve is by car (much more relaxing out of season). At any time of year, try to get off the bad-tempered main EN 125 route. You can also take the train, with vistas infinitely preferable to those from a car. Whatever method you choose, sightseeing is easy because of the relatively short distances involved.

The major attractions are the towns recalling centuries of adventure, triumph, and disaster. Don't miss Faro (see page 36), Tavira (see page 32), Lagos (see page 63), or a day trip to Lisbon (see page 73). Unfortunately, as far as historic monuments go, only a handful still survive from before the year 1755, when almost every building of substance was wiped out by an immense earthquake. Even so, you'll still find vestiges of a vibrant past, and even the humblest village is usually worth a visit with its classic white church, sleepy plaza shaded by vivid blue jacaranda, and, if you time it right, all the local drama of the market.

The Algarve has never had leanings toward sophistication, so don't expect too much in the way of indigenous nightlife. There is not the wide choice of casual drinking establish-

Mending nets is part of a fisherman's daily chores.

ments that is offered by tapas bars in Spain, or pubs in Britain. Much of the evening entertainment is either hotel-based or set up specifically for tourists in cosmopolitan bars and nightspots. But in quieter spots, off the beaten tourist tracks, and in the less commercialized towns, it's easy to meet the locals.

While it is difficult to generalize on the character of the people of such a small region, as a general rule, Algarve folk are rather reserved, yet tend to be tolerant and helpful (ask an Algarvian for directions in the street and you will probably end up being personally escorted to your destination).

Many share the concern that their coastline is being over-developed with indecent haste. But they also know that there are still undeveloped beaches and unspoiled villages to enjoy and that the Algarve still has something to offer everyone.

Algarve's peaceful countryside has the best spots to stop and reflect.

A BRIEF HISTORY

Little is known about the earliest inhabitants of Europe's southwestern extremity. The ancient Greeks called the people the Cynetes, or Cunetes. Whatever their origins, their culture was to evolve under the pressure and influence of foreign forces. Among the many invading armies that contributed to the nascent Portuguese culture were Phoenicians, Celts, Iberians, Greeks, and Carthaginians.

But it was the Romans, who arrived in the third century B.C., who influenced early Portugal most of all. They built towns, industries, roads, and bridges, developed agriculture, imported the Latin language, of which Portuguese is a direct descendant, and named the province Lusitania. In the third century A.D. Christianity was introduced via Rome, and by the beginning of the fourth century the Algarve had a bishop, based in Faro. But Rome was in decay, and soon hordes of northern tribesmen took over the empire. The Algarve fell to the Visigoths in the mid-fifth century.

Snow Place Like Home

You'll never see real snow in the Algarve, but it does have an important place in the region's most charming legend. During the long Moorish occupation, a ruler fell in love with a beautiful slave girl (or princess; versions vary!) from a far northern country. They married but she was deeply homesick, and, pining for the snows of her native land, she fell deep into a melancholy coma.

When the king learned of the reason for her illness, he ordered a forest of almond trees to be planted everywhere in sight of his castle. The following spring he awoke his bride and carried her to the window. The sea of almond blossom had turned the fields snow white and by magic his wife's malaise disappeared.

er Moorish Rule

In A.D. 711, powerful armies of North African Moors launched a devastating attack on the Iberian peninsula. The tide of Islam, which proved irresistible for several centuries, was to leave an indelible influence on the countryside and the population of the Algarve that lives on even today in the form of wells and waterwheels, squat white houses, the complexion and faces of the people, and of course the name itself, a derivation of Al Gharb, which means "western land" (for at that time it was the most westerly country in the known world).

The Moors governed Portugal from across the border in Seville, but the Algarve had its own regional capital, with a vast, red, invulnerable fortress. It was then called Chelb (or Xelb) and was bigger and better defended than Lisbon. Today known as Silves, (see page 51) it is a provincial outpost whose only besiegers are coachloads of tourists.

The long struggle to expel the Moors (the Reconquista or Reconquest) began towards the end of the eighth century A.D., but it wasn't until the 12th century that a significant gain was made. The beginning of the end came in the Battle of Ourique (thought to be near Santarém, farther to the north) in 1139, after which the victorious leader, Count Afonso Henriques, proclaimed himself first king of Portugal.

The reconquest of Silves, achieved 50 years later, was a grisly affair. A mixed bag of Crusaders from northern Europe were recruited en route to their battles east in the Holy Land. They sailed upon the river port of Silves and, ignoring conditional offers of surrender, slew all the inhabitants (at no small loss to themselves) and pillaged the great treasures of the city.

Two years later the Moslem forces rallied again, and Silves again became Chelb. The Reconquista stumbled on for anoth-

Manueline-style architecture, named after King Manuel I, graces many doorways.

er half century. By now there were so many inter-religious alliances, as well as intermingling of Moors and Christians, that it was hard to tell who was on which side and for which piece of land they were fighting. And on top of that, the situation was further clouded by a feud between Portugal and Spain, each of them claiming sovereignty over the Algarve. However, by 1249, Faro and the western Algarve were retaken under King Afonso III and the possibility of war with Spain was averted by an expeditious royal marriage. By the end of the century a treaty with Spain drew up the boundaries of the Portugal we know today.

Recognition that the Algarve was a separate place within the new Portugal came with the title “Kingdom of Portugal and the Algarve.” In those days, the notion of the Algarve as a distinct entity did make some sense. It was after all rather like an island—cut off to the south and west by the Atlantic, to the east by the Guadiana River, and to the north by the mountains. This title was upheld until 1910, when the monarchy itself was overthrown.

The Navigator

In 1415 (long after the Reconquista was complete) a Portuguese fleet assembled on the River Tagus in Lisbon for an assault on the Moors in their homeland. Crossing the Straits of Gibraltar, the armada attacked and seized the North African city of Ceuta. An illustrious member of this famous raid was the young Prince Henry, half Portuguese and half English, the son of King João I and his wife, Philippa of Lancaster. This was to be Henry's one and only military victory, but he was destined to establish Portugal as something of a major world power by helping to develop important world trading routes by the time of his death in 1460.

A glorious scene of old Lisbon in azulejo tiles at the Miradouro Santa Luzia.

At the age of 21, Henry began to assemble his School of Navigation. The form that this school took is an issue of much debate. It was certainly not a formal institution of lectures and classes, and probably resembled an informal modern-day "think-tank." Prince Henry had the money, influence, enthusiasm, and vision to lead and cajole the best astronomers, cartographers, boat-designers, and seamen of the day to roll back Portugal's maritime horizons.

Once sailors were past Cape St. Vincent at far western Algarve, they faced the unknown, with no communications, and no possibility of being rescued if the voyage turned out badly. Yet out into the unknown they went; for the glory of God, country, and themselves, in search of fame and fortune. To this end, Algarve shipwrights developed a successor to the lumbering craft of the day: the caravel. It was light, fast, and manoeuverable; any breeze was enough for a captain to steer it where he wanted to go. With the subsequent development of new navigational techniques, it was no longer neces-

sary to stay within sight of land. Now the only limits to maritime exploration were man's ingenuity and courage.

Tradition says the site of Prince Henry's base is the Sagres peninsula (see page 70), though there is little there today to persuade you of this. The real "mission control" may have been 40 km (25 miles) east in Lagos (see page 63), which had a port, shipyards, and was home to the prince in his role as governor of the Algarve. Wherever and however Henry organised his followers, his achievements are universally acknowledged. During his lifetime, Portugal's caravels sailed

Doing It in Tiles

Just about everywhere you go on the Algarve, you'll see *azulejos* (azoo-lai-joosh)—multi-coloured enamelled tile squares that recall the centuries of Moorish occupation here. Azulejos cover the walls of palaces, churches, humble homes, and park benches alike. The name may originate from the Arab *az-zulayi* (meaning "little stone"). Another school of thought plumps for a simpler derivation from the Portuguese word azul (meaning "blue"), since early tiles were blue and white.

The Moors who brought azulejos to the Iberian peninsula in the Middle Ages may have borrowed the techniques and geometric designs from the Persians. Portugal's first azulejos date from the 16th century. By the 17th century, blue and white were the favoured colours. Some of the finest examples in the Algarve can be seen in churches: São Lourenço (near Almansil, see page 46), the Igreja Matriz at Alte (see page 45), and the cathedral of Faro (see page 36)—all wonderful examples of blue-and-white art. The Igreja Matriz at Alvor (see page 62) uses azulejos in a very different pictorial style.

Other places where you can see a tale of tiles are the palace at Estoi (see page 40), and a Portuguese history lesson given in 10 easy steps on tiled park bench panels in the Largo 1° de Dezembro in Portimão (see page 61).

beyond the most westerly point of Africa. The Atlantic islands of Madeira and the Azores were colonized, laying the foundations for the future Portuguese empire. Before the century was out Henry's compatriots, Bartolomeu Dias and Vasco da Gama, had completed epic voyages, and between 1519 and 1522 another Portuguese explorer, Ferdinand Magellan, led the first expedition to circumnavigate the world.

Foreign Intrigues

In order to protect its seagoing interests and trade routes, Portugal established strategic garrisons in Goa (India), Malacca (East Indies), and Hormuz in the Persian Gulf. Other points of interest around the globe that subsequently felt their influence were Brazil, Macau (now Macao), the Congo, and various other parts of Africa, including the Sudan. The Portuguese policy was to avoid armed strife and to develop a trade empire rather than to conquer nations. To this end it succeeded with relatively few blood-soaked episodes in its colonial history.

Adventures abroad, however, were to prove disastrous during the second half of the 16th century. In 1557, the popular 14-year-old boy-king Sebastião ascended the throne. Thus began a calamitous reign that was to end at the battle of Alcacer-Quiber (Morocco) in pursuit of a vain crusade. Sebastião's untimely demise, alongside some 18,000 ill-prepared, badly led followers, set the stage for a crisis of succession. For many years afterwards, legends and rumours bizarrely insisted that the king was still alive, and imposters turned up from time to time claiming the throne; those who were plausible enough to be deemed a threat were summarily executed.

In fact, the only rightful claimant to the crown was the elderly Prince Henry. But after two years of alternating between the throne and his sick-bed he died, heirless.

Surveying the situation with a certain amount of glee, Spain moved in to fill the power vacuum, and Portugal's neighbour and long-time antagonist became its master.

Among the unpleasant aspects of Spanish rule was Portugal's inadvertent involvement in Spain's wars. In 1587, a squadron of British ships that were commanded by Francis Drake, attacked the Algarve (now a "legitimate target" as Spanish territory) and sacked Sagres, thus depriving the world of the relics of Henry the Navigator. Nine years later Faro was put to the torch—all a far cry from the Treaty of Windsor in 1386 under which Britain and Portugal had pledged eternal friendship.

During this period, Portugal's empire was gradually eroded, with many of its trading posts (with the notable exception of Brazil) being picked off by the British and Dutch. Finally,

Prince Henry the Navigator, with sextant in hand, still charting the waters off Lagos after 500 years.

after 60 years of Spanish rule, Portuguese noblemen (aided by the French, who were then at war with Spain) organized a palace coup and restored independence.

The Great Disaster

Portugal's greatest ever misfortune struck on All Saint's Day, 1 November 1755. With the candlelit churches crowded, a huge earthquake struck. Those not immediately killed by falling masonry had to contend with fast-spreading fires and then a devastating tidal wave, which swept over the Algarve inland as far as 6.5 km (4 miles). The exact casualty figure will never be known, but it is estimated that 5,000 died immediately and between 40,000 and 60,000 perished as a result of secondary injuries and the ensuing famine and pestilence. The epicentre of the earthquake is thought to have been off the Algarve coast, possibly between Tavira and Faro. Witnesses claim to have seen a fiery volcano erupt from beneath the sea just before the first jolt.

Throughout the Algarve and much of the rest of southern Portugal, virtually every important monument, cathedral, castle, and mansion was destroyed, or at least critically damaged in the earthquake. Among the hardest hit towns was Lagos (see page 63) which lost its castle, all its churches, and the palace in which Henry the Navigator had once lived.

Political Upheaval

The turn of the 19th century brought further shudders to the country. This time the epicentre was Paris, and the cause was Napoleon. Just as Portugal's (forced) alliance with Spain had made her a target for Drake's 16th-century raids, so now her (friendly) alliance with England rankled with Napoleon.

In 1807, the French invaded Lisbon and the royal family fled to Brazil. Spain, followed by Portugal, rose up against

Old and new chimneys intermingle in this Albufeira skyline. Only television aerials tell you it's the late 20th century.

the French occupation, in what came to be known as the Peninsula War.

Among the early blows struck for independence was a rebellion in the town of Olhão (see page 28). On 16 June 1808, the townsfolk—armed with little more than ancient swords, spears, and stones—attacked and captured the local French garrison. It's said that a party of local men then set sail in a fishing caïque from Olhão all the way to Brazil, without any maps or navigational aids, to tell the king of the insurrection. The real battle, however, was waged under the leadership of the Duke of Wellington, whose coalition forces expelled the French after two years of bitter fighting.

The war left Portugal further weakened, and in 1822 its major empire outpost, Brazil, declared independence. At the same time, a dispute over the crown continually raged between

Pedro IV, the absentee monarch who preferred to hold forth as Emperor of Brazil rather than return to Portugal, and his brother Miguel. The power struggle, with strong overtones of absolutism versus liberalism, excited the interest and intervention of other powers. With British help, Pedro defeated Miguel off Cape St. Vincent in 1833, and his expeditionary force marched to Lisbon. Pedro took the throne, though armed struggle continued for months and the bitterness long after that.

By 1892, Portugal, racked by wars and the continuing expense of maintaining all its African colonies (including those of Mozambique and Angola), declared itself bankrupt. The seeds of discontent with absolutist rule were well and truly sown.

Kingdom's End

Bloodshed was to haunt the remaining years of the Portuguese monarchy. On 1 February 1908, the royal family was riding in an open carriage along the Lisbon river-front, Terreiro do Paço, when an assassin opened fire and killed King Carlos. A fellow gunman in the crowd simultaneously despatched the heir to the throne, Prince Luis Filipe. His younger brother, Prince Manuel was also hit, but survived and was thus propelled to the throne at the tender age of 19.

Amid republican agitation, however, he was deposed in 1910 in a surprise uprising

An architectural detail of a typical Lagos home.

led by elements within the armed forces. Having ruled for less than three years, Manuel died in exile in 1932 in England.

The sudden end of more than seven centuries of monarchy brought a great deal of confusion and crisis to the country. Presidents and prime ministers hopped into and out of office an unbelievable 45 times between 1910 and 1926, until a revolution by the military suspended Portugal as a democracy. After six years of power, General Oscar Carmona appointed his brilliant finance minister, António de Oliveira Salazar, to be Prime Minister—a position he was to hold until 1968. The tough, austere, inward-looking dictatorship of Salazar put the Portuguese economy back on its feet, though little else of any merit came out of it. Portugal remained neutral during World War II, and Salazar demonstrated his financial acumen by selling materials to both sides.

In 1968 the elderly Salazar was forced into retirement after a stroke. His successor, Dr. Marcelo Caetano, feeling the spirit of the age, began tentative relaxations of the old regime but did not go nearly far enough. The armed forces finally overthrew him in a popular bloodless coup on 25 April 1974.

Portugal now began to pull out of the long and fruitless struggle against revolutionaries in its African colonies and granted independence to the last of its empire. This, too, caused major upheavals, and a million permanent refugees returned to the motherland, aggravating the shortage of housing and jobs.

Although economic problems still beset the young democracy, the past few years have seen a general stabilization of the political scene, and in 1986 Portugal joined the European Community.

Since then, the Algarve has received funds to build up its infrastructure and to invest in tourism. Meanwhile, the rest of Portugal aims to build up its industrial and agricultural resources.

WHERE TO GO

The Algarve is a small place. As your plane touches down at Faro, just 50 km (30 miles) separates you from Spain to the east, and it is only 112 km (70 miles) west to *o fim do mundo* (the end of the world) at Sagres. Along this 160-km (100-mile) coastal strip, several resorts and holiday villages of every kind have sprung up, so wherever you are based, you'll never be far from a good beach, a reasonable size town, village, or resort, shops, and nightlife.

We've divided the Algarve into six areas (with an excursion to Lisbon as well), each of which may be seen in a day's outing, though of course you may wish to stay overnight to sample the atmosphere and the character of the towns and villages. We begin in the east.

Look out for the brightly painted gypsy carts off the beaten track.

THE SOTAVENTO COAST

As you head east from the provincial capital of Faro (see page 36), the first settlement of any size you will come to is the  colourful fishing town of **Olhão.** This is a working port that has made few concessions to tourism, and it is full of character.

Olhão has often been described as the "little white Cubist town of the Algarve," and its architecture likened to that of North African towns. This certainly was the case some years ago, but modern development has strongly interfered with its once distinctive appearance. You can judge

Reading the Map

Finding your way around the Algarve is easy, provided you master a few essential words. Here's a list of most of the words you're likely to come across during your explorations:

avenida	avenue	*miradouro*	belvedere, viewing point
barragem	dam	*mosteiro*	monastery
Câmara Municipal	Town Hall	*paço, palácio*	palace
capela	chapel	*parque*	park
casa	house	*ponte*	bridge
castelo	castle	*praça*	square, plaza
cidade	town	*praia*	beach
claustro	cloister	*rio*	river
convento	convent	*rua*	street
cruz	cross	*saída*	exit
entrada	entrance	*sé*	cathedral
escada	stairs	*torre*	tower
fortaleza	fortress	*tùmulo*	tomb
igreja matriz	parish church	*turismo*	tourist information office
largo	square		
mercado	market	*vista*	view

for yourself by ascending the bell tower of the **Igreja Matriz** (parish church), which you will find by winding your way through the narrow streets back to the Praça da Restauração (you may have to ask for access to the tower in the sacristy). Instead of the red-tiled roofs and filigreed chimneys seen elsewhere in the Algarve, the Olhão skyline comprises flat-topped roofs of terraces called *açoeitas*. Look hard and you can still see the narrow, outside staircases leading to whitewashed towers, where fishermen's wives, or perhaps smugglers, would look out for the incoming fleet.

The name of the square, Restauração ("restoration"), recalls Olhão's most glorious moment, when an improvised local army rebelled against Napoleon's occupying forces in 1808 (see page 21). This insurrectionary zeal subsequently spread throughout the rest of Portu-

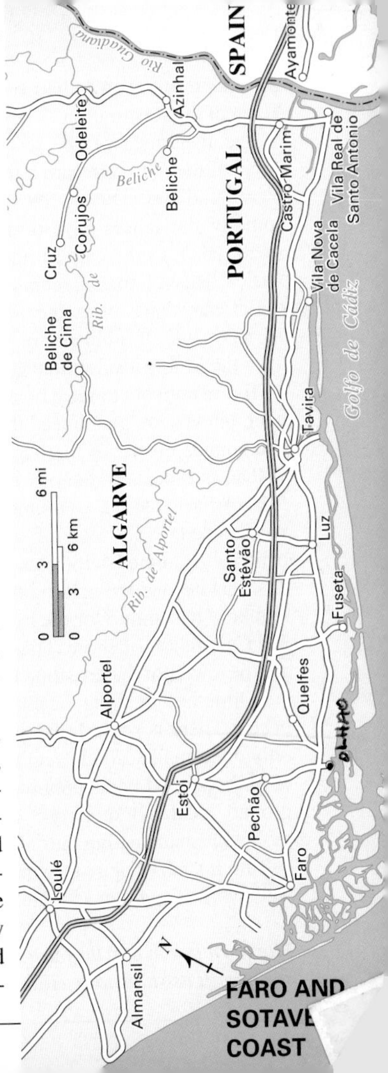

gal and resulted in Olhão being awarded the title "Noble Town of the Restoration."

The fishermen of the town have a hardy reputation—some of them used to earn a living in cod waters as far off as Newfoundland. During the past two centuries, however, some of the sailors have turned away from fishing and instead, taken to the cargo trade between Portugal and North Africa. This relatively recent link with the neighbouring continent may have been the inspiration for the local North African style of architecture. In any case it developed long after the Moors had left the Algarve.

You're unlikely to see a boat coming in from another continent, but you are guaranteed the hustle, bustle, sights, smells, and sounds of one of the Algarve's best daily **fish markets** (Olhão is especially famous for its mussels and other shellfish). Adjacent to the voluminous market buildings are small, well-tended parks, one of which boasts several splendid benches decorated with blue-and-white *azulejos* (see page 20). Just beyond the park on the other side, ferryboats depart regularly in summer for the barrier-island beaches of Armona and Culatra just offshore. These lovely, undeveloped **beaches** are the jewels of the coastline between Faro and Tavira.

A little farther along the coast at **Fuseta** is another popular beach. There is some holiday development here, but as yet only on a small scale. Fuseta itself is little more than a creek of gaily-painted boats bobbing at anchor, while in the background local workers rake salt crystals into small white mountains punctuating the saline delta.

Turn inland, because the small village of **Moncarapacho** is well worth the 8-km (5-mile) detour. A fine old church, a

The town beach of Albufeira has graced a thousand postcards with its sandstone cliffs and beautiful waters.

sleepy village square, and a local museum await you. The countryside around here is full of orange and almond groves and, as you head east (back on the main road) towards Tavira, olive groves and vineyards also start to appear. Tavira's grapes produce a good, rustic wine that is drunk all over the Algarve.

After the salty flavour of Olhão and the rural serenity of Moncarapacho, the aristocratic bearing of **Tavira** may come as something of a surprise. This tuna-fishing port and spacious, self-assured town of historic churches, imposing classical-style mansions, and riverfront gardens probably goes back as far as the Phoenicians or the Carthaginians—and its seven-arched stone bridge of Roman origin is still in use. Head straight for the town hall, with its imitation medieval arcades, and pick up a town map and leaflet from the tourist information office. Just across the street are the old castle walls, which you can climb for the best overall view of the city.

There are over two dozen notable churches in Tavira but, conveniently, the best two are within a few metres of each other. The **Igreja de Santa Maria do Castelo,** built into the castle, is not to be missed. The Gothic portal is the only original 13th-century part of the building to have survived the devastating 1755 earthquake (see page 23). In the chancel is the large tomb of Dom Paio Peres Correia, who drove the Moors out of Tavira in 1242. Just down the hill is the beautiful 16th-century **Igreja da Misericórdia**, with a fine 18th-century interior. A lively fruit and vegetable market is held by the banks of the river, and it is well worth crossing the bridge to view more of the town's elegant houses and pretty flower-filled squares. After a morning of exploring the town, you can take a boat to one of Tavira's offshore beaches, or to Fuseta.

East of Tavira lies the fledgling resort of Manta Rota and the well-established, high-rise canyons of **Monte Gordo.** The reason behind all this development is a huge sandy

beach which stretches for some 10 km (6 miles) between the two resorts and is backed by pine trees and dunes. Although it's not the most attractive of the Algarve's resorts, the comprehensive beach and watersports facilities at Monte Gordo are enough to satisfy any tourist, and by night a casino is the focus of attention.

The Guadiana River, which runs into the Atlantic 3 km (2 miles) east of Monte Gordo, was a natural frontier for 2,000 years, forming the boundary between the Roman provinces of Lusitania (Portugal) and Baetica (southern Spain). This explains the strategic importance of **Castro Marim,** a former fortress town rising from the flatlands to command the broad river. For five centuries its primitive castle-fortress was occupied by the Moors. After the Reconquest it became the home of the new Military Order of Christ (succeeding

Tavira offers gracious, classical-style buildings and cool, well-tended gardens — an aristocrat among Algarve's towns.

The town of Vila Real de Santo António was built to impress the Spanish just across the river.

the disbanded Knights Templars). Look for the inscription inside the main entrance proclaiming that Prince Henry the Navigator, who was a governor of the order, once lived here. These days the castle itself is in need of defence and restoration, and although it may no longer be of any military value, its broad, unpolluted marshlands do attract large numbers of wading birds. The area is protected by the National Parks service and is very popular with birdwatchers.

A little to the south, the town of **Vila Real de Santo António** (the Royal Town of St. Anthony) was designed to be as grand as its name suggests in order to impress the Spanishon the other side of the river. The town plan was the inspiration of the Marquês of Pombal, the dynamic hatchet man of King José I, and the town was built from scratch in just five months in 1774. To appreciate just how important the marquês once was, visit Lisbon, where you'll see his statue looking down over the city from his column at the top of the Avenida da Liberdade.

The town square, **Praça do Marquês do Pombal,** is the work of the royal architect, and the tour de force of Vila Real. The pavement consists of black and white wedges of stone that radiate from an obelisk in the centre of the square in a sun-ray effect. Distinguished three-storey, late 18th-century houses line the square, and orange trees soften the edges, adding colour and scent. Visit the small Manuel Cabanas Museum, just off the square, to see a fine collection of woodcuts that ranges from rustic scenes to famous statesmen and composers.

Aside from the bullring, Vila Real de Santo António's main appeal is as the ferry port to **Ayamonte** across the water in Spain. The trip takes just 20 minutes—less time than it would take to drive to and over the new bridge—and the white town of Ayamonte is a fine sight as you approach it from the river. You will need to take your passport.

Fishy Business

Any night, out on the ocean, 2 or 3 km (a mile or two) beyond the beach, you may see tiny specks of light glinting below the stars. These are the lanterns of a small fleet of fishing boats in a wide formation, luring fish into an elaborate net structure. For centuries fishing has been big business in the Algarve, but the biggest boom began 100 years ago when the canning industry came to the region. To this day, thousands of tons of fish, mostly sardines, with tuna coming in a close second, are caught, tinned, and exported annually.

Those who have tasted the "real thing" fresh from the quay at Portimão (see page 59), or elsewhere in the Algarve, can only feel a little sorry for those who have to take their pleasures many weeks later, from a tin!

FARO AND UPLANDS

Faro, the provincial capital of the Algarve, is also the area's most discounted town. Most tourists fly into Faro, go directly to their resorts, and only return two weeks later to fly back out. Those who return to explore find a very different atmosphere from that pervading some of the resorts on the coast. Faro is a friendly and welcoming town, with a picturesque old quarter. Tourists are welcome but never a stifling presence in the authentic Portuguese restaurants, cafés, and bars.

Faro was always an important town, even during Roman times, when it was allowed to coin its own money. It continued to thrive under the Arabs; its name may be a derivation from the name *Harune,* one of the old city's ruling families. It was retaken in 1249 and prospered until 1596, when an English fleet commanded by Queen Elizabeth I's favourite, the Earl of Essex, plundered and burned it, as part of Spanish territory. Until comparatively recently, when the area silted into a tidal flat, Faro was a commercial and fishing port open to the Atlantic. Indeed, the Earl of Essex's fleet was able to sail right up to the city walls. Nowadays small fishing boats and pleasure craft have to zigzag carefully amid the dunes and then creep beneath the railway bridge to enter the sleepy harbour.

Signs: ***entrada livre*** **–**
admission free
é proibido tirar fotografias **–**
no cameras allowed

The main entrance to the **old town** is the 18th-century **Arco da Vila**, alongside the tourist information office. This charming arch and bell tower is perfectly topped by a venerable family of nesting storks. Beyond the arch, the cobbled street, worn shiny by centuries of tramping feet, leads up to the splendid, wide-open Largo da Sé (Cathedral Square), at its best in the evening when floodlit and free of cars. The unusual cathedral

Faro's former convent, the Convento de Nossa Senhora da Assunção, is home to the Algarve's loveliest cloister.

tower (along with the main portico) is part of the original 13th-century Gothic building. Inside are some fine examples of *azulejos* (see page 20).

No less impressive than the cathedral is the **Convento de Nossa Senhora da Assunção** (Convent of Our Lady of the Assumption), which contains the most beautiful cloister in the Algarve. Abandoned as a convent in the 19th century and then put to improbable use as a cork factory, it has now been beautifully restored as a museum devoted to archaeology, the **Museu Arqueológico e Lapidar Infante Dom Henrique.** The principal exhibit is a 2,000-year-old Roman floor mosa-

This statue graces the Estoi Palace.

ic measuring 9 metres (30 feet) long and 3 metres (10 feet) wide. Unearthed in Faro, it depicts a bearded sea-god, although unfortunately the bulldozer that discovered it in 1976 shaved off the lower half of his face. Displays of Portuguese art are housed in the many rooms off the cloister.

The real attraction of Faro's old town, however, is not its set-piece buildings, but the quiet, hidden, timeless atmosphere of its tiny houses, narrow, cobbled alleyways, and such establishments as the friendly Café do Largo, where classical music accompanies your coffee.

In the centre of town, the cobbled and shaded municipal **Jardim Manuel Bivar** is a popular meeting place for young and old alike, complete with open-air café and an old-fashioned bandstand. As in several other Algarve towns, the main shopping area is pedestrianized, and cafés and restaurants spill out onto the street, fish displays and all.

The **Museu Etnográfico Regional** (Regional Ethnographic Museum) is at the top end of the main shopping street, Rua de Santo António. Here you'll find good displays of local handicrafts, reconstructions of rooms in a typical Algarvian house, and atmospheric old photographs of the region. Note the colourful water-cart that Manuel Ignacio Miguel of Olhão operated for 60 years, almost up to his death in 1974. He travelled the region selling fresh water in huge pottery jars, until the modern supply network put him and his donkey out of business.

Faro boasts several fine churches, but the best is without doubt the **Igreja do Carmo** (Carmelite Church). The promise of its Baroque towers and stately façade is matched by a beautiful interior, but the greatest attraction, seemingly, is its macabre Capela dos Ossos (Chapel of Bones). This 19th-century curiosity employs the skulls and bones of parishioners, or monks (depending on who is telling the story) as construction material.

Other churches worth a visit include the Igreja de São Francisco (open for services only), and the former chapel of Igreja de Santo António do Alto. The latter, at the very top end of town, houses a small religious museum, but the real attraction is its tower, which commands a fine view over the

The Manueline Style

During the reign of Manuel I (1495–1521), artists were inspired as never before by the discovery of far-off lands and the romance of daring sea voyages. The style they evolved, called Manueline after the king, celebrated this brave new age of maritime travel. Motifs such as anchors, knotted ropes, sails, terrestrial globes, marine plants, and animals became the signatures of this period's sculptors and architects.

The most famous example of Manueline art is considered to be Lisbon's marvellous Belém Tower (see page 77), but you can also see exuberant stonework all over the Algarve. Look out for the church portals and windows at Silves (the Igreja da Misericórdia, page 53), Alvor (see page 62), and particularly at Monchique (see page 55).

whole of Faro (check with the local tourist information office on opening hours).

It is well worth spending a night or two in Faro. Watch the sun setting over the fishing boats in the lagoon while you have a drink in the splendidly old-fashioned, cavernous Café Aliana (the meeting place for everyone), or eat at an outdoor restaurant. There are also some lively music bars.

Faro also boasts a good **beach,** the Praia de Faro, noted for its watersports. You can drive there across the single lane causeway linking the long, strip of dunes with the mainland (no buses or motorhomes allowed), or in the summer catch a ferry from the pier by the old town. If the ocean is rough, simply cross to the opposite side of the sand spit and swim in the calm, warmer waters of the lagoon (though be aware it can sometimes be muddy and a little unpleasant).

Signs:
***entrada* – entrance**
***saída* – exit**

The Algarve is not famous for historical sites due to the 1755 earthquake that destroyed so much (see page 23), so it is a bonus that two of them should be so close to each other, just a few miles from Faro. The first, and by far the most impressive, is the 18th-century **palace of Estói.** You'll find it by driving to the village centre and walking through a small side gate just to the left of the church steps. The charming Baroque house, which once belonged to the Dukes of Estói, is small in palatial terms, and only its garden is open to the public. But there is plenty to see; balustraded terraces and staircases with splendid bursts of bougainvillaea, busts of historic characters impaled on the parapets, brightly coloured wall tiles, and formal gardens. Both the palace and gardens are currently being restored.

The dusty **ruins of Milreu** are 1.5km (1 mile) down the road from the village. Like the palace of Estói, Milreu was once the large country house of an eminent person, though in this case he was Roman and pre-dated Estói by some 1,400 years. The knee-high walls that trace the outline of this once luxury establishment are still clearly visible. The tall, semi-circular tower ruin is thought to have been a temple to pagan water gods at one time; however, by the fifth century it had clearly been converted to a church.

Head north for 7 km (4 miles) through fertile farming land of almonds, carobs, and olives and you will reach the market town of São Brás de Alportel. To get an overview of the town, drive past it, following the signs to the pousada (a government-sponsored inn, like a Spanish parador). The view from the terrace here stretches over much of the surrounding

A filigreed chimney in contrast with a brightly coloured rooftop in Salir.

countryside, and it's also a good place to stop if you want to try some authentic regional cooking.

It's best to visit the town on Saturday, when the lively **market** transforms its otherwise sleepy character. Do also pay a visit to the charming **Museu Etnográfico do Trajo Algárvio** (Museum of Algarvian Costume), where changing exhibits of local dress are well staged in a large, old house 90 metres (100 yards) or so off the main square.

From São Brás, the flower-lined road to **Loulé** passes through rolling orchards of fig, olive, and orange trees. Like São Brás, Loulé is a regional produce centre with a Saturday market, but on a much larger scale, and is also known for its leather, lace, and copper goods. Loulé is a prosperous town with an ambitious, modern boulevard complete with outdoor cafés that are jam-packed on Saturday. Coach parties come from far and wide to shop at the colourful, bustling market.

Actually there are two markets. Fresh produce, including fish, is sold in a mock-Moorish hall, while a "gypsy market" is held towards the opposite end of the boulevard. Just below the permanent market halls, on the main Praça da República, you'll find a well-preserved section of the medieval **castle walls.** This offers excellent views from the town, and set into the castle remains is a local museum. In the streets directly below the walls, you may well hear the sounds of craftsmen beating copper. Watch them and buy direct. It may not be that much cheaper than buying from a shop, but at least you will have had the satisfaction of seeing your purchases made. You can also see artisans at work on the pottery wheel, producing leather goods (such as decorated saddles and bridles) and furniture. The craftsmen of Loulé are said to be the descendants of a community of Moslems who found refuge in the district at the end of the Reconquest (see page 16). If you are in the Algarve in springtime, don't miss the Loulé Carni-

Religion is a part of everyday life and special occassions, as seen in this procession in São Brás de Alportel.

val. The parades, "Battle of Flowers," and musical celebrations are the best of their kind in the region.

As you head farther north, the whole way of life becomes visibly slower and more rustic, with bonneted ladies in black by the roadside, old men on donkeys, bright gypsy carts, and families out knocking almonds from the trees with their long sticks.

The pretty village of **Salir,** northwest of Faro, is built on the edge of a steeply rising ridge and has two fine lookout points. The first is in the village itself, alongside the 16th-century parish church and water tower (don't miss the delightful gardens next door). The other, with the best views, is the adjacent peak, which once held a Moorish stonghold (follow signs to the Castelo). All that remains of the castle are the bases of four huge turrets (12th–13th century) and some excavations and the old castle grounds are home to a tiny hamlet, complete with its own church. The panoramic views across to the main part of Salir and the surrounding countryside are spectacular, and there is even a tiny *miradouro* (belvedere) café here.

As charming as Salir is, it merely whets the appetite for **Alte**—possibly one of the Algarve's most picturesque villages. It is entered in idyllic fashion, across a small, white bridge over a babbling stream that descends to and through town, and waters a rich valley thick with oranges, pomegranates, and figs.

Follow the stream upriver and you come to the popular Pequena Fonte (Little Fountain) restaurant where folk-dancing draws the crowds. Despite the name, there are no fountains here (just springs), but the setting is delightful and a perfect spot for a picnic.

Getting around on pony is actually not an uncommon means of travel.

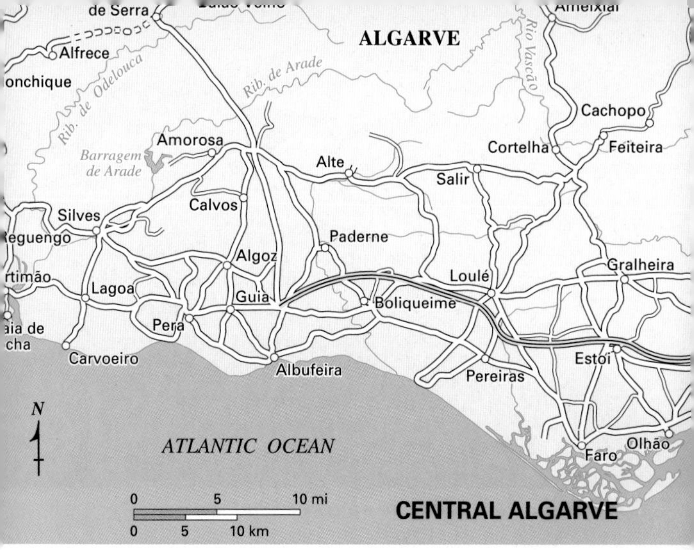

The architectural highlight of the village is the beautiful 16th-century **Igreja Matriz,** entered through a classic Manueline portal. The church keeper will enthusiastically point out the many elaborate chapels and the rare 16th-century Sevillana *azulejos* (see page 20). The rest of Alte is the Algarve of postcards—white-washed houses along narrow streets, colourful windows, filigreed chimney pots, and red-tiled roofs. And while the character may at first seem uniform, you won't see two houses the same.

WEST FROM FARO

The terrain changes west of Faro from the long flat beaches of the east to the rugged, rocky lines of the Barlavento coast. You wouldn't know it from the main highway or the railway line, though, as they run parallel to the coast several miles inland and out of sight of the sea.

The dramatic cliffs and waters of São Rafael.

As you leave Faro and join the EN 125 route heading west, look for an isolated roadside building with two mythological dragon-like monsters in relief. This, known as the **Casa das Figuras** (House of the Figures), is the old storehouse for a farm that long ago occupied this now-empty site.

Some 16 km (10 miles) west of Faro, a simple white church stands out on a small hill overlooking the thundering highway. Slow down or you'll miss it—the sign says "S. Lourenço"—**São Lourenço** (St. Lawrence). The interior of the church is the ultimate in classic *azulejo* design. Almost every square inch of its walls and its vaulted ceiling is covered with tiles up to 250 years old depicting biblical scenes. The only relief from the blue and white is the gilt, carved altar. Cottages next to the church house exhibits of contemporary Portuguese art.

Farther west is the small crossroads town of **Almansil,** with shops, cafés, and businesses, many of which are dedicated to the comfort of the English expatriate (English speaking real-estate offices and the Pig & Whistle pub-restaurant, for example). Many of these ex-pats live just a few miles south on the coast, and it is here that two of the Algarve's most luxurious holiday developments are found. Surprisingly, given their status, neither Quinta do Lago nor Vale do Lobo are well sign-posted off the main road.

A little farther west, **Quarteira,** once a sleepy fishing village, has also been developed and is now a busy resort with a long, golden beach. Parts of the old town have survived the tourist onslaught, however, and there are good, cheap restaurants in the old quarter where locals and adventurous visitors mingle. The municipal **market** still stands on the beach; every Wednesday one of the largest and busiest markets on the Algarve—offering fish and produce—is held next to it. Generally, there is room enough for both locals and tourists here; fishermen and fishwives tote live lobsters, tourists tote Nikons, and the two contingents eye each other with great bemusement.

Filigreed Flues

Tourism has often been called the industry without chimneys—but not so in the Algarve, where its graceful, lattice creations, reminiscent of Moorish lanterns, have become a trademark of the region. For hundreds of years, Algarve house-owners have taken great pride in the beauty and originality of their chimneys, and it is said that the more elaborate the chimney-pot, the wealthier the owner. Originally they were carved of wood, then they became ceramic, and latterly concrete. The area in and around Faro in particular enjoys a strong reputation for its rooftop art, but keep your eyes skyward and you'll see pretty chimney pots all over the Algarve.

Nearby **Vilamoura,** known as Europe's biggest-ever private tourist undertaking, has been planned down to the last designer café, 19th-hole club bar, and the Algarve's biggest **marina,** the main object of attention in the area and a bright addition to this part of the coast.

The marina designers were not the first to take advantage of Vilamoura's harbour. The Romans built a dock in the same place and established an important fishing centre here. The remains of the **Cêrro da Vila** centre were unearthed across the road from the marina. Aside from some low-level excavations showing the elaborate water-piping system and surviving mosaics, there is also a small museum displaying everything from fishhooks to lamps, appealing to any student of archaeology.

West of Vilamoura the coastline begins to feature the dramatic rock formations that have made the Algarve so famous. **Olhos de Agua,** the first important resort on this part of the coast, is in many ways typical of the genre. A single road leads down between pine-covered cliffs to an intimate, soft, sandy beach shared by a small, gaily painted fishing fleet, curiously eroded sandstone formations, and sunbathers. The resort derives its name from the "eyes of water" which flow from strangely formed rocks visible only at low tide.

There are more excellent beaches at **Santa Eulalia** (longer and more open than Olhos de Agua), **Balaia, Praia da Oura,** and São João. The latter two are regarded as satellites of Albufeira and may well be where you are staying on a package holiday to Albufeira. The centre of activity along this beach hinterland is the infamous "Strip"—a long street leading up to the hilltop area known as Montechoro. This is lined with a motley collection of bars, restaurants, and nightspots.

Albufeira, at one time a picturesque fishermen's town, has managed to preserve a small amount of its traditional charm in spite of being developed on a vast, commercial scale. It would be difficult to ruin its magnificent setting—enormous, pockmarked sandstone cliffs rise above a huge beach lined with colourful fishing boats and hundreds of sunbathers. The gently sloping sands are perfect for family holidays, and if you are looking for a little more privacy you can escape the crowds by heading farther east along the sandy coast. A tunnel links the centre of the town with the main beach.

As the tractors haul the fishing fleet ashore, the sunbathers leave their towels to gape at the **catch**—1 metre (3 foot) eels, still flapping; foot-long, spiny lobsters still snapping; and various indistinguishable types of flat and silver fish by the bucketload. The famous beachside **fish market** gave way to the inevitable logistics problem some years ago and moved just

In Moorish times, Silves was the most powerful city in the Algarve.

Monchique is a popular village; its most famous monument is this Manueline-style portal.

north of the centre. It is still worth a visit, however, and you will also find fruit, vegetables, and flowers on sale.

Albufeira's name suggests a Moorish connection—the Moors named it Al-Buhera ("castle on the sea"). Its cliff-top position and labyrinthine street plan provided an easily defensible spot for the Moors, and this was one of the last towns to fall during the Reconquest. Its layout, however, did not save it from the 1755 earthquake, during which it was almost completely destroyed.

Modern Albufeira has fallen to the acolytes of mass tourism —international bars, cafés, and nightspots pump out music day and night. There is little that is traditionally Portuguese about its raucous central square, but in spite of this it has retained its charm, and there are quiet spots to be found. Furthermore, wherever you are in the striking maze of white houses, you're never far from the Atlantic, and from almost any vantage point the view of Albufeira and its seascape is spectacular.

In Largo Jacinto d'Ayet, a modern **statue** honours a native son of Albufeira. Vicente de Carvalho, an Augustinian friar, was arrested in Japan during a time of Christian persecution in 1632. The statue portrays his martyrdom—he was burned at the stake in Nagasaki and beatified in his native Portugal in 1867.

With so much activity to the east, the excellent beaches west of town are relatively uncrowded. The best are **São Rafael,** a beautiful, sandy strip with some splendidly shaped rocky outcrops, and Coelho and Castelo, two small, beautiful coves.

SILVES TO THE SUMMIT

Once upon a time, over eight centuries ago, **Silves** was a magnificent Moorish city of palaces, gardens, bazaars, and a huge red castle on a hill. While Granada boasted the legendary *Alhambra,* the Algarve too had a city straight from the Arabian Nights.

Taking the Waters

They say one sip of the waters at the Monchique spa (see 55) will add 10 years to your life span. The 15th-century Portuguese king João II evidently believed this, as he visited the spa in an attempt to cure his dropsy. Unfortunately it didn't significantly extend his life, and he died at Alvor soon afterwards. If you can't sample this "eau-de-vie" straight from the source, try the bottled version. You'll see the Monchique label whenever you ask for an água in any bar on the Algarve.

Sailing ships carried the treasures of the East up the busy Arade River from the Atlantic; its wealth was renowned so far afield that it even attracted the unwelcome attention of the Vikings. Today that same great river, where the Moors fought off the Norsemen, is a sluggish, silted shadow of its former self. Gypsies bathe among a few weary rowing boats, and the town has become a backwater, as evocative as a rusted old treasure chest.

But while the riches of Silves were stolen long ago, the glorious setting remains. The old, white town climbs up the hillside from the river, its medieval bridge still intact, and is surmounted by a large red-coloured fortress. Look down from the castle and you will see mile after mile of orchards—oranges, lemons, grapefruit, clementines, and pomegranates.

The Golden Age of Silves began in A.D. 711 with the Moslem invasion. The occupying forces made the city, then called Chelb (or Xelb), the capital of the Algarve. With redoubtable fortifications and a population in the tens of thousands, it was one of the strongest outposts in 12th-century Arab Iberia. The city was attacked and taken by the Crusaders in 1189, recovered by the Moors two years later, but finally lost in the Reconquest of 1242 (see page 16). The loss of Arabic wealth and the silting up of the River Arade left Silves almost literally high and dry, and by the time the bishopric of the Algarve was transferred to Faro in 1577 its population had dwindled to 140 men, women, and children.

Silves has had a **castle** of sorts since Phoenician times. The Romans built a version, and the present castle took shape after the Reconquest, though its lines are still very Moorish. It has been lovingly restored, with oleander and jacaranda to soften the warlike mood, and there are fine views over the tiled roofs of the town and surrounding countryside.

Next to the castle is the impressive Gothic **Sé** (Cathedral) of Silves, built by the liberating Crusaders, some of whom are buried within. Much restored after vandalism, earthquake, and time itself took their toll, it still retains a majestic air. The remains of a Moorish mosque are hidden behind the altar. Opposite is the 16th-century **Igreja da Misericórdia,** with a classic Manueline-style side door (see page 39).

Wander down to the main square, the Praça do Municipio, and the imposing **Torreão das Portas da Cidade** (barbican) will give you a good idea of how seriously the defence of the Arab city was taken. You can see inside this sturdy, warlike structure, as it now houses the peaceful mu-

Nothing compares to the tiny beaches found in Nossa Senhora da Rocha.

The beach at Lagos.

nicipal library and is open free of charge. Close by on Rua das Portas de Loulé is a brand new modern **archaeology museum.** Here you can see part of a large Arab water cistern and other local finds.

Today, Silves is having a resurgence as the centre of a prosperous farming region, and it enjoys some of the benefits of tourism without flaunting itself as a day-tripper's town. Its streets are a delight to wander at random, and you can finish off your tour with a drink down by the riverfront.

Just outside the city, on the road to São Bartolomeu de Messines (route N124), is an important 16th-century religious sculpture. It depicts the crucifixion of Christ on one face and His descent from the cross on the other and is known as the **Cruz de Portugal** (Cross of Portugal). This small, weather-beaten 3-metres (9-foot) high statue which can easily be missed, is only really of interest to aficionados of religious art.

If you are travelling by car, continue to the **Barragem** (dam) **do Arade.** The water collected in this reservoir surrounded by pine hills provides irrigation for the area's profitable orchards. It's a refreshing spot, perfect for a picnic as well as sailing and windsurfing.

Most organized excursions combine a visit to Silves with a trip to Monchique and Caldas de Monchique (two separate villages), then on to Foia, the highest point of the Algarve. The first stop on this scenic, leafy, journey is the spa village of **Caldas de Monchique,** known since Roman times for its therapeutic waters. Its heyday was the Edwardian era, and many of the elegant buildings (including a casino and a handicrafts market) still date from this period. Aside from a few tourist shops, little has changed since then, and once the coaches have rumbled on, a melancholy air of nostalgia rolls back over this sleepy hollow.

This is also a good place for a picnic and a stroll in the woods. If you don't get a chance to taste the water here, you can drink it (carbonated or still) by the bottle in any bar or restaurant in the Algarve.

North from Caldas, the road weaves uphill very quickly, rising 300 metres (1,000 feet) in 5 km (3 miles) past terraced farmlands and forests of eucalyptus, oak, and cork. **Monchique** is a small market town, known for its handicrafts and the famous Manueline doorway of its **Igreja Matriz** (see page 39). Compared to Caldas and Silves it lacks character, but you can buy home-made nougat, hand-carved wooden utensils, and straw goods. High above the town, the ruins of a 17th-century convent loom like a ghostly grey eminence.

The road continues ever upwards, passing roadside souvenir and fruit vendors, and several idyllically placed *miradouro* restaurants. At the end of the line is **Foia,** almost 915 metres (3,000 feet) above sea level, affording one of the best **views** in Portugal. There is no settlement here, just a collection of craft and souvenir stalls, a bar, a restaurant, and an obelisk marking the highest point on the Algarve. On a clear day you can see from the bay of Portimão to the Sagres peninsula (see page 70), and pick out the rocky outcrops of the Lagos beaches.

Although you may welcome a breeze after the heat of the coast, the wind blows pretty sharply at Foia, so you'll need a sweater. Don't worry if you've forgotten to bring one; the best buys among the souvenirs here are the chunky hand-knitted cardigans and pullovers.

WEST FROM ALBUFEIRA

The beach of **Armação de Pêra** is one of the longest in the Algarve—a flat, golden stretch to the east, picturesque rock stacks and small coves to the west. By contrast with the lovely beach, the development to the east end of town has unfortunately not been in the best taste and has all but eclipsed the former fishing village. On the front, however, there is a pleasant esplanade and a small fortress, built in 1760, which contains a pretty chapel.

West of Armação de Pêra, development along the clifftops continues apace. However, the vast majority of apartments and villas here are low-rise, and perhaps because the road system is not fully developed here, this part of the coast has largely escaped the attentions of mass tourism.

One of the most photographed beaches along this stretch is **Nossa Senhora da Rocha** (Our Lady of the Rock). The rock in question is a promontory, boldly jutting out into the sea, surmounted by a little white fishermen's church. To either side of the rock are two lovely coves. Back inland, just before the main road is the pretty village of **Porches**, with some classic, white Algarvian houses and filigreed chimneys.

Porches is famous for its **pottery,** though you won't find much in the village itself. Get back on to the EN 125 route and cross it almost immediately to get to the first pottery shop, Olaria Pequena, a small workshop turning out excellent, high-quality earthenware. Farther along the road is its parent, Olaria, and then a little farther still the Casa Algarve, which sells pottery and handicrafts in an attractive old house with some interesting antiques and large-scale *azulejo* panels (see page 20).

Boat trips are the only way to see the rock formations of the Barlavento coast, such as at delightful Carvoeiro.

Lagoa, a sizeable town, is well known throughout the Algarve for its wines, and is the province's wine capital. The *vinho da casa* served in most restaurants on the Algarve comes from here. Lagoa wine, both red and white, is more powerful than ordinary wine, and the extra degree or two of alcoholic content can creep up on you. The local tourist office can arrange tours of wineries and tastings. (Don't confuse Lagoa, pronounced lah-go-ah, with the historic port town of Lagos (see page 63), pronounced Lah-goosh, about 19 km/12 miles to the west).

From Lagoa, turn south about 5 km (3 miles) to the charming resort of **Carvoeiro.** The beach appears to be the size of a tablecloth compared with some of the expanses to the east—this is the archetypal small Barlavento resort. A single road runs down through a pretty valley until it comes to a small crescent of sand shared by sunbathers and fishing boats. Above, rows of bright, white houses perch on red sandstone cliffs while cafés and restaurants fill the spaces in between. The original village of Carvoeiro is now fairly commercialized, but while there are some who mourn the loss of its innocence, to many people it is still one of the coast's most attractive resorts.

A narrow road follows the cliffs eastwards to the geological curiosity of **Algar Seco** ("dry gully"). Wind and wave erosion have created here, among many other weird and wonderful shapes, a double-decker stone arch. There are walkways down to a lagoon enclosed within the menacing rocks, and if the weather conditions are calm this open-air grotto is a true paradise for snorkellers.

Fuel types for cars/trucks: unleaded (*semchumbo*), premium (*super*), diesel (*gasoleo*)

Continue on east and you will find three more beaches like Carvoeiro, whose relative isolation has thus far protected

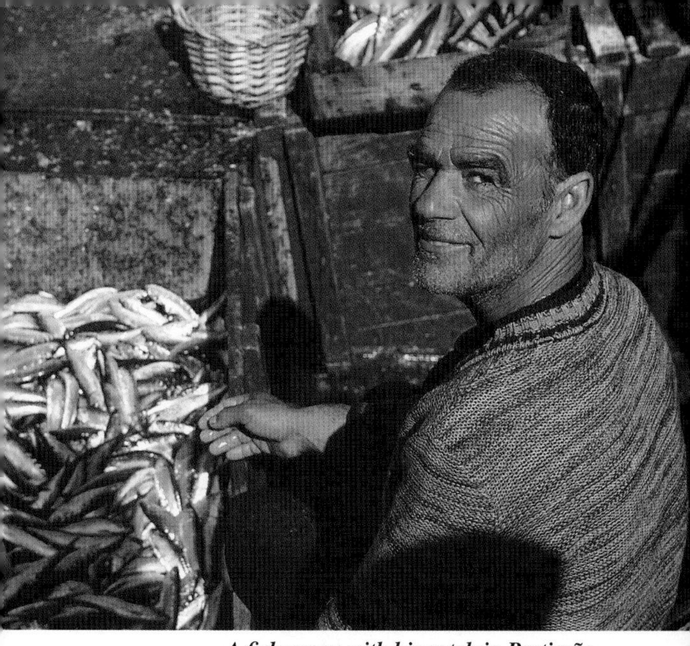

A fisherman with his catch in Portimão, "the sardine capital of the world."

them from development. They are (heading east) **Vale de Centianes, Praia do Carvalho,** and **Praia de Benagil.** This last in particular is superb, and is approached down a vertiginous road flanked by massive cliffs.

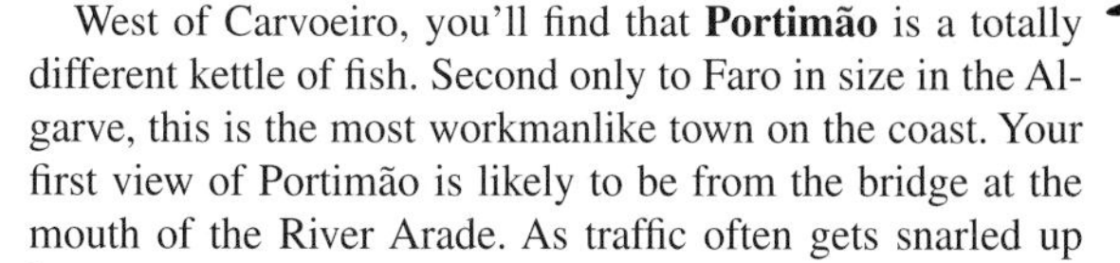

West of Carvoeiro, you'll find that **Portimão** is a totally different kettle of fish. Second only to Faro in size in the Algarve, this is the most workmanlike town on the coast. Your first view of Portimão is likely to be from the bridge at the mouth of the River Arade. As traffic often gets snarled up here, you may get a longer look than you strictly need.

A view of the splendid beach and fantastic rock formations at Praia da Rocha.

If you are at the town end of the bridge and it is near lunch or dinner time, you will probably catch the heady aroma of grilled sardines. The centre of activity is almost directly beneath you on the **dockside** where the "Sardine Capital of the World" does its most to earn its nickname. If you have just one meal in Portimão, have it here, and make it sardines. Presentation is entirely ignored, but the taste is as good and the prices are as low as anywhere you'll eat on the Algarve.

The hectic operations of the fishing industry used to take place here right under the noses of holidaymakers, with a frenetic "bucket-brigade" hauling wicker baskets of fresh fish up from the boat holds to icetrays and waiting lorries, right next to dockside dining tables. Logistics and the demands of tourism have now pushed the fishermen to a larger location on the other side of the river, but most sightseeing boats include a quick trip to the new docks on their agenda. You will still see fishing boats at anchor on the main quay, but the majority of river traffic here now is pleasure craft—smart private yachts, replica sailing ships on tourist excursions, and tiny dinghies cutting across the waves.

After all the colour of the dockside activity, Portimão town suffers a little by comparison. As one of the Algarve towns damaged the most during the earthquake of 1755, it has very few buildings or monuments of any historical interest. Perhaps to compensate for this, the town fathers have constructed the **Largo 1° de Dezembro** (opposite the tourist information office), a park with ten splendid blue-and-white *azulejo* benches, each illustrating a pivotal event in the history of Portugal. The park's name comes from the date, 1 December, 1640, when Portugal's independence from Spain was restored (see page 22).

Walk up Rua Pimenta to the centre of town and you will come to the attractive Igreja Matriz church. Across the square, directly in front of the church, is the old market building, now used for temporary art exhibitions. There is more art across the street (next to the Igreja do Colégio) housed in a small gallery and museum.

Portimãio's other claim to local fame is as a comprehensive regional **shopping** centre. There is certainly a good range of shopping here, including many international names, although there are a few outlets selling traditional crafts or locally made items.

Praia da Rocha has a long history as a holiday village for wealthy Portuguese families and was "discovered" by the

British in the 1930s. Then, this quintessentially Algarvian "beach of the rocks," strewn with the most extravagantly shaped formations, provided an inspirational refuge for writers and intellectuals.

Today the long, 2km (1¼ mile) golden **beach** is as good as ever, and the main attraction, but what was once a village behind the beach has unfortunately been developed with new hotels and yet more tourist facilities. Vestiges of the village's former grandeur can still be traced along the front, where grand old buildings jostle uncomfortably with burgeoning high-rise blocks. These now stretch so far back as to completely blur Praia da Rocha's separate identity from Portimão.

At the very eastern end of the resort, guarding the River Arade, is the **Fortaleza de Santa Catarina** (St. Catherine's Fortress), built in 1621 to defend Silves and Portimão against the Moors. Little remains of the actual fortress, but its courtyard is now a very agreeable terrace where you can enjoy a drink and watch the sardine fleet returning to port. Directly across from the fortaleza is the splendid beige-coloured Fortaleza de Ferragudo (closed to the public). On closer inspection, by boat, you will see that it bears an uncanny resemblance to a giant sandcastle.

The old fishing village of **Ferragudo** nearby is well worth a visit. Despite its proximity to much tourist activity, and boasting two excellent beaches of its own, it refuses to become too commercialized and remains a traditional fishermen's settlement. The opposite end of Praia da Rocha's long stretch is known as Praia do Vau. The rock formations and coves continue, but this end of the beach is quieter and less developed than the eastern end.

Alvor, to the west, is a classic Algarvian fishermen's village. Narrow cobbled streets plunge downhill to a quay and market where boats bob at anchor on a wide, marshy lagoon. A handful of *tascas* and bars rustle up sardine barbecues every bit as rustic as those you'll find at Portimão. At the top of the hill is a charming 16th-century church with a much-admired portico carved in flamboyant Manueline style (see page 39), and some excellent *azulejos* in the chancel (see page 20). Concessions to tourism include the huge white-sand beach—the main focus of a recreational area including a golf course and a casino.

TO WORLD'S END

Lagos is one of those rare towns that offers something for everyone. By night it is often lively while still retaining a

The Foolish King

Of all the statues in the Algarve, none provokes so much comment and probably none caused so much controversy when it was erected (in 1972), as the figure of King Sebastião in Lagos. Sebastião was a 16th-century boy-king, but you'd never guess it from this memorial. The figure here resembles more an androgynous astronaut than a medieval monarch; garbed in a clingy silver-foil suit with modern bikerstyle gauntlets, a bright, flesh-coloured, girlish face peeps out from beneath what appears to be an ill-fitting toupée.

One of this young, charismatic king's first acts was to make Lagos the capital of the Algarve, which no doubt won him this statue. But it is for his final decision that he is most remembered. Flying in the face of military advice, he led 500 ships and 15,000–18,000 ill-prepared men from the beach of Meia Praia to conquer Morocco. Only a handful returned.

Latter-day Sebastianists probably see the modern statue as a fittingly flamboyant memorial to a brave monarch; those less charitably inclined no doubt view it as an aptly ridiculous epitaph to a disastrous leader. See it on Praça Gil Eanes and make up your own mind.

peaceful façade; by day it combines a rich historical past with a busy present. Its main beaches are just slightly out of town, so it is not a classic resort in the mould of Armação de Pêra or Praia da Rocha. This may well be Lagos' saving grace—for many this is the best all-round town on the Algarve.

Your first view of Lagos will probably be from the long, riverside Avenida dos Descobrimentos (Avenue of the Discoveries), which divides the old walled city from the port. Cross the river to watch the busy fishermen and you will also be rewarded with a fine **view** of the city rising above the walls. In contrast to the wide, busy avenue in front of you, many of the streets towards the top of the town are narrow, cobbled, and more used to donkeys than to the internal combustion engine. The town still retains much of its walls intact; part Roman in places, it has, however, been much rebuilt and expanded over the centuries. Climb them for fine views over the port and out to sea.

The Moors made Lagos an important trading port, but it was after the Reconquest that the town enjoyed its heyday. It was proclaimed the capital of the Algarve, and the governor's palace became the headquarters of Prince Henry. A fine **statue** of Henry, seated with sextant in hand, has been erected on a plaza, next to the main avenue. Arguments persist over the exact whereabouts of the prince's School of Navigation, but it seems almost certain that Lagos was the principal shipyard and port serving his team of explorers.

An unfortunate result of the explorations along the west coast of Africa in the mid-15th century was the establishment of the slave trade. Lagos was a key player in this trade in human misery. Just behind the statue of Henry, on the corner of Rua da Senhora da Graça, you can still see the small **arcade** where Portugal's first slave auctions took place. Black captives were tied to the metal posts of the arcade to

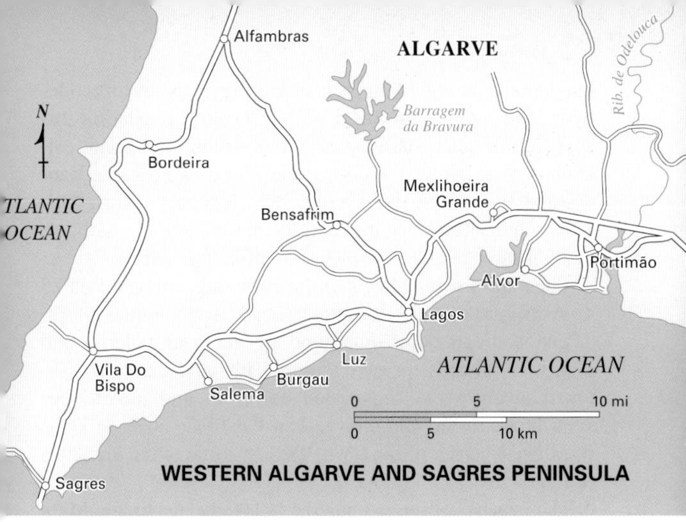

await their new life at the hands of the highest bidder. A small plaque simply says "Mercado de Escravos" (slave market). Most of the other historic buildings that stood hereabouts were tragically lost in the devastating earthquake of 1755 (see page 23).

One survivor of the Golden Age is the chapel of the **Igreja de Santo António,** an exuberant gilt Baroque work that King Midas would have been pleased with. Figuratively as well as literally down-to-earth is the floor tomb of an Irishman, Hugh Beatty. He was a soldier of fortune who commanded the Lagos regiment of the Portuguese army in the late 18th century, and must have been held in very high esteem to have been awarded such a prestigious final resting place.

There are plenty of other curiosities to explore next door in the **Museu Regional de Lagos.** Sacred art, archaeological remains, the original charter of Lagos, holy vestments, donkey halters, an eight-legged goat kid preserved in formaldehyde, and many more local objects jostle for space in this eclectic, old-fashioned museum. For a more up-to-date collection, visit the neat, well-restored Forte da Ponte da Bandeira at the end of the Avenida dos Descobrimentos. This 17th-century fort once guarded the entrance to the harbour; in addition to its museum pieces, it offers fine sea views.

The main street of Lagos is the charming, cobbled Rua 25 de Abril, packed with restaurants, bars, and antiques shops. The side streets hold some good art and craft galleries and plenty of rewards for exploration. Tiny cafés, an old-fashioned bakery with a fine period storefront, and an Art-Nouveau kiosk by the old city gate at the Praça João de Deus (northwest corner of the town) are just some of the vignettes of Lagos life.

The beaches of Lagos span the full Algarvian range. **Meia Praia,** 1.6 km (1 mile) to the east, is a long (4 km/2 ½ mile) flat stretch which, out of season, can be quite empty. By con-

Saintly Odyssey

Cabo de São Vicente, or Cape St. Vincent, is named after a fourth-century Spanish priest martyred by the Roman governor of Valencia. When the Moslems invaded Iberia, the saint's body was taken as far west as possible, to the Algarve's "Sacred Promontory." Eventually this too was overrun by the Moors, and the holy relics disappeared.

After the Reconquest, however (see page 16), Afonso Henriques, first king of Portugal, sent out a search party to find the remains. Legend has it that they were guided to their hiding place by a pair of ravens, and as the ship sailed back to Lisbon with the saintly bones, it was accompanied by the birds. The seal of the city of Lisbon commemorates the legend with a sailing ship and black birds fore and aft.

Lagos, once the capital of Algarve, is the most complete town in the region.

trast, the beaches just west are the archetypal pocket handkerchief-sized coves. The weird and wonderful rock formations, as well as the steep cliffs, have marked them as some of the most photographed in Europe; head for **Dona Ana** and **Praia Camilo** in particular.

At the southern tip of the coast, just before it turns west to Sagres, are the most spectacular rocks of all. The **Ponta da Piedade** (Point of Piety) is a stunning family of rock bridges and grottoes. Every other stack and cliff formation you may have seen on the Algarve up to now has been a mere appetizer. There is no beach here, but summer boat trips depart from the foot of the long stairways that have been cut deep into the sides of the cliff.

For a complete change of scenery, take a drive northwest towards **Bensafrim.** Here you can enjoy the old Algarve of

rolling undeveloped countryside, where people still make a living off the land. The tilled soil, a startling ochre colour, makes a colourful backdrop for orange and lemon groves. Turn off towards the **Barragem** (dam) **da Bravura** and you'll be rewarded with a sight that is every bit as inspiring as its name. This picturesque water, more akin to the English Lake District than sunny southern Europe, is also of great practical use, irrigating crops, including rice, around Lagos. To the west of Lagos, a new road complements the old EN 125 route and will undoubtedly open up this relatively undeveloped area.

The first resort west of Lagos (10 km/6 miles) is **Luz,** a pleasant seaside town. All that remains of old Luz is the church and (opposite) the **fortress.** The latter has been attractively renovated and turned into a restaurant. There is a good beach with watersports facilities and large, flat rocks where holidaymakers bask, lizard-fashion.

Burgau, 3.2 km (2 miles) west, is smaller and sleepier than Luz. Fishing boats pulled up onto the end of the road leading down to the beach jostle with cars in what resembles a bizarre traffic jam. The beach here is not as attractive as those at neighbouring Luz or Salema, but the small village retains its character and could be a good choice for a quiet holiday.

Salema is regarded as the "up-and-coming" resort of this stretch, with a lively sprinkling of bars and restaurants, a pleasant beach with fishing boats, and a market.

The last settlement of any size before Sagres is **Vila do Bispo.** Take a break in the pleasant, flower-garden square and pay a visit to the 16th-century church. Its walls are cov-

The heart of the sacred promontory. It is said that Prince Henry charted his voyages using this compass.

ered with 18th-century *azulejos* and its ceiling decorated with frescoes.

Sagres has strong historical connections, not least with Henry the Navigator, and an impressive view over the fishing harbour and beyond to some good beaches, one of which has a first-class watersports centre. Beyond the village of Sagres, a great, rocky peninsula hangs above a brooding ocean. Since time immemorial the mood of this forlorn place, known as the Sacred Promontory, has stirred the imagina-

An aerial view of the red and white rooftops of Lisbon.

tion. It was once believed to be a sleeping place of the gods. If a man wanted room to think, he'd have plenty of time and space on this plateau, far from distractions. Which may help to explain why Henry the Navigator may have chosen this site for his 15th-century School of Navigation.

As you approach the grey bulk that was Henry's **fortress** (actually more of an observatory), its sheer size seems to dominate the horizon. Unfortunately, inspection at closer quarters reveals somewhat insensitive restoration work. In 1991, the 18th-century walls of this nationally important monument were re-faced with stark, unrelieved grey concrete in a move which won few friends and destroyed all the external character of the building, and the same can be said of new construction within the fortress. Its principal building, that may have been Henry's headquarters, has been demolished. Today there remains only one original building, which houses a tourist information office, and a chapel (open for services only).

Frustrated English tourists who would like to have learned more about Prince Henry may do well to consider that even before 1991 Sagres had been a virtual ruin following its destruction in 1587 by Sir Francis Drake.

The other evidence that attests to Henry the Navigator at Sagres is a huge stone **Venta da Rosa** (rose compass) on the floor of the compound, measuring 39 metres (130 feet) in diameter. If you ascend the stairs by the compound entrance, you will also find a tiny sundial on the corner of the wall overlooking the compass; how these may have aided the great voyages is unknown. A modern shell in the castle grounds houses an exhibition room.

En route to Cabo de São Vicente (Cape St. Vincent), stop at the remains of the **Fortaleza do Beliche.** This small, attractive 17th-century castle still houses its tiny, white, domed chapel and is also home to a smart traditional-style restaurant and an annexe for the pousada in Sagres. The rough, white-stone castle walls here are how those of Sagres appeared before they were restored (see page 71).

The cliffs of **Cabo de São Vicente** signal journey's end, and to ancient mariners it was more besides—*o fim do mundo* (the end of the world). This intensely bleak spot was

Museum Finder: Five of The Best

If you only have a day or two to explore Lisbon, you probably won't want to spend too much time looking at museum collections. However, some of them are quite special and could well be worth an hour or so of your time, particularly if it's raining (all of these museums are free on Sunday and closed on Monday):

Ancient Art Museu Nacional de Arte Antiga, Rua das Janelas Verdes. The most important national collection of Portuguese paintings.

Coaches Museu Nacional dos Coches, Praça Afonso de Albuquerque, Belém. One of the largest and most valuable coach collections in the world.

Decorative Arts Museu Escola de Artes Decorativas, Largo das Portas do Sol, Alfama. Old palace full of choice pieces from the 15th to 19th centuries.

Folk Art Museu de Arte Popular, Avenida Brasília, Belém. Country crafts and folk art.

Gulbenkian Collection Museu Calouste Gulbenkian, Avenida de Berna at Praça de Espanha. One of the world's biggest private collections—Egyptian, Islamic, and Asian art, Flemish tapestries, Old Masters, French fine art, and plenty more.

the last sight of Europe for those explorers setting forth on marathon voyages into the unknown. Today, as both supertankers and small yachts heave into view around the cape, it all seems very different. But looking down from the cliff, even on the calmest of days, you can sense the cataclysmic force stored in the Atlantic. The lighthouse, built in 1846 (not open to the public), with its beam visible up to 96 km (60 miles) away, is at the tip of the point. This is one of the few points along the Algarve where you won't be tempted to take a dip.

EXCURSION TO LISBON

Until the 19th century, the overland journey from the Algarve to Lisbon, Portugal's capital, took a week or more. Now it's only half a day by road or rail, and you can fly from Faro in just 40 minutes. If you only have a couple of days to spend in Lisbon, however, you may like to consider an all-inclusive coach excursion from the coast, which takes care of accommodation and sightseeing.

For many years Lisbon has enjoyed a reputation as a relatively quiet, easy-going sort of town, lacking the hustle, bustle, and general hassle of other major European cities. But while this is still true to a degree, the gap is now closing and Lisbon is becoming altogether more European. None of which should put you off a visit.

Underground fare in Lisbon is the same irrespective of the distance you travel.

The centre of Lisbon is small, compact, and easy to get round in two or three days. Moreover, it boasts two charming old quarters which are as characterful as those anywhere in Europe. If, however, you intend staying in Lisbon for longer than two days, it is well worth touring the surrounding region. The popular Estoril coast, including

Cascais, and the beautiful hilltown of Sintra are two of the most popular excursions.

Exploring Lisbon

The city is built on hills—by legend seven, in fact many more—but the great thing for the visitor is the splendid vantage points and lookouts that these provide. The best place to start your tour of Lisbon is from the **Castelo de São Jorge,** the king of all view-points. From here you can look out over the whole of the city and along the broad, majestic Rio Tejo (River Tagus), spanned by the longest suspension bridge in Europe.

The castle is set just above Lisbon's most famous *bairro* (district), the **Alfama.** Here you will discover a labyrinth of narrow, crooked streets, winding, cobbled alleyways, decaying old houses, former palaces, fish stalls, and bars totally unknown to tourists. Little has changed here in decades, if not centuries.

There is another marvellous view of the town from the charming park, **Miradouro de Santa Luzia,** just down the hill from the castle. Close by is the Sé (Cathedral) of Lisbon with its ancient, cavernous interior. In addition, there are reckoned to be at least another dozen first-class churches in the city, including the lovely Igreja de Santo António da Sé (adjacent to the Sé).

Two other churches of note are the **Igreja do Carmo,** devastated in the earthquake of 1755 and deliberately preserved as an atmospheric ruin in memory of it, and, nearby, the sumptuous Igreja de São Roque. Both churches also feature museums, and can be found in the Bairro Alto.

Brightly coloured flowers on display in Lisbon's main square, the Rossio.

Like Alfama, the **Bairro Alto** (high district) is a hilly area full of evocative houses that are decorated with wrought-iron balconies usually occupied by birdcages and flowerpots. At night the district is loaded with exciting atmosphere and is famous for its *fado* clubs (see page 89). It's a relatively harmless place by day, but you should be on your guard if visiting after dark. You can walk to this area easily from the central squares, but it's also fun to go by tram or instead to board the landmark 30-metre (98-foot) Elevador de Santa Justa, which you'll find just off the Rossio. This 1902 Victorian marvel of iron and glass was built by Raul Mesnier. The longer, slower way back downhill meanders through the upmarket shopping area of **Chiado**, where just looking can be almost as much of a treat as buying.

The Tower of Belém silhouetted in the sunset.

Lisbon's main square is the Praça Dom Pedro IV, better known as the **Rossio,** and just to the north is another square, **Praça dos Restauradores.** Look out for the giant horse-shoe-shaped doors of the railway station here. The city plunges steeply downhill to the River Tagus and its most imposing square, **Praça do Comércio**, lined on three sides by gracious arcaded buildings and a vast triumphal arch. Nearby, one of Europe's largest aquariums, the Ocean Pavillon, floats on the Rio Tejo.

Some 6 km (4 miles) west of Praça do Comércio lies the riverside district of **Belém.** It was from here that the age of exploration (begun on the Algarve) reached its zenith between 1497 and 1499, when Vasco da Gama's voyage to India opened up a major new sea route. During the following century, Portugal enjoyed a golden age of trade, and King Manuel celebrated the discoverers with two magnificent monuments.

The most famous is the small but exquisitely formed **Torre de Belém,** as romantic a medieval fortress as you will ever see (particularly by night, when it is magically floodlit). By contrast the majestic **Mosteiro dos Jerónimos** is Lisbon's biggest religious monument and a truly formidable example of Manueline architecture (see page 39). The church and its double-decker cloister survived the 1755 earthquake, and in addition to royal tombs holds the relics of national heroes Vasco da Gama and the poet Luis de Camões. The monastery also houses the **Museu Nacional de Arquelogia e Etnologia,** and next door is the **Museu da Marinha** (Naval Museum). There are two more museums at Belém; the **Museu de Arte Popular**, dealing with folk art and customs, and the highly popular **Museu Nacional dos Coches** (National Coach Museum), which is located in the former riding school of the Belém Royal Palace.

One final sight in Belém is the very modern **Monument to the Discoverers**. This huge, splendid waterfront sculpture depicts Prince Henry the Navigator at the prow of a stylized caravel that juts into the Tagus River. The figures behind represent noted explorers, map-makers, and astronomers whom Prince Henry mobilized in order to launch Portuguese ships into the history books.

Estoril Coast

Excursions follow the coast west from Lisbon, as the riverfront evolves into a series of Atlantic Ocean beaches. The most famous is **Estoril,** a resort about 24 km (15 miles) from Lisbon. This cosmopolitan area was a haven for deposed European royalty in the first half of this century. Victorian villas and modern mansions can be glimpsed behind barriers of shrubs, vines, and trees. The casino, located at the top of the gardens of the Parque do Estoril, combines a night-club, restaurants, bars, exhibition hall, and cinema, along with a gambling operation that is big enough to keep some 200 croupiers busy.

In contrast to Estoril's formality, **Cascais** is a happy combination of a still-working fishing port, a residence for aristocrats, and a tourist resort. Overlooking the main swimming/fishing beach, the 13th-century citadel is one of the few buildings to have survived the earthquake and tidal wave of 1755.

Sintra

Finally, excursions turn inland to the fetching hill town of **Sintra.** Since the 14th century, Portuguese kings have made the **Paço da Vila** here their summer home. This royal palace (closed on Wednesday) right in the centre of town is topped by two gigantic conical chimneys. When you tour the build-

The Monument to the Discoverers, which decorates a fortress on the waterfront in Belém.

ing, you'll discover they are the kitchen ventilation shafts, vital in the days when oxen were roasted for banquets.

The **Palácio da Pena** is a far more extraordinary dwelling. It is most impressive viewed from afar, when it resembles a Gothic fortress. Up close it turns out to be a mixture of architectural styles (Gothic, Manueline, Renaissance, and Moorish) and is actually a folly built by a German Baron in 1840.

The **view** from here is extraordinary. From a height of 457 metres (1,500 feet) you can see all the way from Lisbon to the Atlantic, which is exactly what the kings who took residence here wanted it for.

On a nearby hilltop, the **Castelo dos Mouros** (Moors' Castle) dates from the eighth and ninth centuries. Its conquest by the forces of Count Afonso Henriques in 1147 was considered a pivotal triumph in the Reconquest of Portugal.

WHAT TO DO

SPORTS

The Algarve has long been famous for its golfing facilities, and latterly some former big names in British tennis have also taken advantage of the favourable climate to set up schools here. And with around 160 km (100 miles) of south-facing beaches, there is also plenty of scope for watersports enthusiasts.

Watersports

Most of the larger beaches have equipment for hire, but don't count on expert tuition everywhere. Aside from the main beach resorts there are good facilities at Praia da Luz (where the Sea Sports Center is Algarve's leading watersports center), the marina at Vilamoura, the lake and beach at Quinta do Lago, and at Praia da Martinhal, Sagres.

Fishing

The waters of the Algarve provide some of the best big-game fishing in Europe. Shark (mostly blue, but occasionally copper, hammerhead, mako, or tiger), marlin, billfish, large bass, and giant conger are regularly hauled in. Swordfish and tuna can be caught farther out. Portimão, Sagres, and Vilamoura are the main centres.

Take a break and sail away to Praia da Luz.

If the deep sea doesn't appeal, you can rent a boat, rod, and reel. Or just a rod and reel to use off the rocks at a harbour entrance, or off the cliffs. Angling conditions are generally best in the winter, from October to mid-January.

Jet-skiing

For more high-speed fun on the water you can jet-ski at Praia da Rocha, Quarteira, Alvor, or Quinta do Lago, or hop aboard a "water-banana" (a banana-shaped inflatable towed behind a speedboat) and skim the waves at Armação de Pêra and Praia da Oura.

Sailing

Dinghies and instruction are for hire at Praia de Luz, Quinta do Lago, and Portimão, and sailing also takes place on the picturesque dam, Barragem do Arade (see page 55). For bigger craft try the marina at Vilamoura or the Carvoeiro Club. Anchorage as well as harbour facilities are available at Lagos, Faro, Olhão, Portimão, Sagres, and Vila Real.

Scuba-diving

The Luz Bay Sea Sport Centre, the longest established diving club in Portugal, offers daily dives from Praia de Luz, exploring the wonderful grottoes and rock formations between here and Lagos. You can of course also explore this remarkable coastline with a good snorkel and mask. Other centres include Atlantic Diving at Praia dos Aveiros, Albufeira, and Clube Torpedo at Vilamoura.

Water-skiing

Not so popular on the Algarve, partly because of the rough nature of the Atlantic and also due to spiralling costs. Try Sagres or Quarteira. The protected lagoons that stretch from Quinta do Lago to Manta Rota provide good, calm waters.

Windsurfing

This is the most popular watersport along the Algarve coast, and you'll find good tuition at Praia da Rocha, Ferragudo, Praia da Luz, Praia de Faro, and Quinta do Lago. The last two are particularly flexible as they have both sea and sheltered water and can therefore provide calm conditions if that's what you require.

Sports Ashore

Golf

There are 14 major golf courses on the Algarve, many designed by the biggest names in the sport. All boast luxury clubhouses, manicured greens, and immaculate fairways.

Hole number 7 at Vale do Lobo. Hook here and you'll be in the sea.

The top courses are to be found clustered around Vilamoura and stretch west to Lagos. Many golf facilities are currently under construction. The best (from west to east) are:

Parque da Floresta (Budens, near Salema): 18 holes. A spectacular rolling hillside course offering excellent value.

Palmares (near Lagos): 18 holes. A course with ocean panorama plus high hills and deep valleys which provide quite a challenge.

Penina (near Portimão): 36 holes. The longest and oldest Algarve course, with a distinguished championship history. Waterways and lakes are a predominant feature.

Vilamoura 1 (near Quarteira): 18 holes. Laid out along the lines of the classic English courses; narrow fairways between umbrella pines create testing conditions.

Vilamoura 2: 18 holes. Magnificent sea views and small greens which demand accurate approaches.

Vilamoura 3: 27 holes. With water hazards on eight holes and heavy bunkering around the greens, precise and accurate iron play is called for.

Vale do Lobo: 27 holes. A rugged terrain with fine views, culminating in the "most photographed hole in Europe"; a spectacular par 3 stretching 192m (210 yds) over two cliff ravines above the sea. Fairly narrow fairways penalize careless drivers.

Vila Sol: 18 holes. Thought to have some of the best fairways in the Algarve.

Quinta do Lago: 36 holes. One of Europe's finest courses. American-designed with outstanding lush greens and roomy fairways—water is the biggest hazard.

San Lorenzo (near Quinta do Lago): 18 holes. A new but already established course in a beautiful setting.

For more details of facilities, write to the Portuguese National Tourist Board for a copy of their excellent golfing brochure, *Sportugal.* Keen golfers should also consider the option of accommodation at a "Golf Hotel." Typically these are establishments very close to the top golf courses which offer free (or heavily discounted) golf on courses that may otherwise be difficult to get a game on. They also arrange golf tournaments among their guests.

In addition to the above, if you don't want to play a full round then there are also several mini-golf courses.

Horseback Riding

Whether you're looking for pony rides for children, treks for the competent, or hacks for the inexperienced, the mixed terrain of beaches, rolling hills, and woods makes riding in the Algarve a delight. The Pine Trees Riding Centre at Quinta do Lago is highly regarded and offers a friendly and professional service. Also consider Horses Paradise at the Paradise Inn in Almarcil. Also recommended are the schools at Vale de Ferro (Mexilhoeira Grande between Lagos and Praia da Rocha) and at Vale Navio (Albufeira).

Tennis

The most prestigious complex on the Algarve is the centre at Vale do Lobo, which boasts 12 all-weather courts (continually being expanded), including six which are floodlit. Close by is the very well equipped Vilamoura Tennis Club, with several courts. Another famous centre is run by David Lloyd at Rocha Brava near Carvoeiro, with 10 all-weather courts, of which five are floodlit. The neighbouring Carvoeiro Clube de Ténis also has 10 courts.

Other hotels with a good number of courts include the Alfa Mar, Praia da Falésia, near Olhos de Agua (18 courts); Hotel Alvor Praia (7 courts); and Hotel Montechoro, near Albufeira (8 courts). Tuition in the pleasant surroundings of the Ocean Club at Luz (3 courts) is demanding but rewarding.

SHOPPING

The shops of the Algarve are well stocked with trinkets and souvenirs, but if you're looking for genuine handicrafts or local goods, try the regional markets. These colourful affairs, sometimes referred to as gypsy markets (due to gypsy patronage), are a mixture of everyday wares for local consumption, genuine local handicrafts, leather goods, and clothing. Usually held once or twice a month in the larger regional centres, they are popular with locals and tourists alike.

Another option is to go direct to the artisans' workshops. These are becoming increasingly difficult to find, as when the old craftsmen retire, their descendants are now turning to tourism instead of the traditional ways. Loulé and Monchique are probably your best bets.

Sizes (medidas) may vary. Make sure to try on shoes and other clothing before you buy.

What to Buy

Azulejos: Colourful and handpainted glazed tiles are about as Portuguese as you can get, and will certainly liven up your kitchen or patio. But remember that they can be heavy to carry home.

Brass, bronze, and copper: Candlesticks, pots and pans, old-fashioned scales, bowls, and trays, and even small stills for distilling your own gin can be found. *Cataplanas* (see page 95) make a delightful decorative or functional souvenir.

Confectionery: Marzipan and figs are the basis for typical Algarve sweets, so you'll need a super-sweet tooth to enjoy them. They are often produced in brightly coloured animal or fruit shapes. Look out for them in Lagos (see page 63).

Pottery from Porches — probably the prettiest purchase in this part of Portugal, and also an excellent value.

Cork: Portugal is the world's leading producer of cork. It comes in the form of placemats, intricate sculptures, and other designs, and is ideal for luggage weight-watchers.

Embroidery: You won't have to look hard for embroidered tablecloths; they'll be thrust upon you by gypsy street sellers. Haggling is the name of the game. Look out for the delicate needlework of the island of Madeira.

Knitwear: One of the region's few genuine bargains, so think ahead to winter at home. Stalls at the suitably windy venues of Foia and Sagres are surprisingly good value.

Leather: These goods are no longer at basement prices, but bargain shoes, handbags, etc., can still be found. Smart shoe shoppers should shuffle along to Portimão.

Port: crusty old vintages of Port can still be found in dusty bottles, but they are expensive and hard to find (see page 97).

Pottery: Excellent choice and value from tableware to gardenware. Porches is the best place to visit (see page 57).

Rugs: Mostly from the Alentejo region (north of the Algarve), as beautifully hand-made as they've been for centuries.

Wicker: Bags, mats, furniture, plant-holders, glass-holders, trays—you name it, they'll sell it to you.

EXCURSIONS

Tour operators run various day trips by coach to several destinations, including Lisbon, Seville, Monchique and Silves, and Sagres and Cape St. Vincent. Two options that are a little different (and more difficult to do by yourself) are a **river trip** up the River Guadiana along the frontier between Portugal and Spain, and a jeep safari that explores the mountain roads where only four-wheel-drive vehicles can go.

Boat trips exploring the nooks and crannies of the famous Barlavento coast, always a popular choice, depart from several points west of Vilamoura, most notably from Portimão. Vessels fashioned after old-time sailing barques hoist their sails once at sea and are a fine sight. Day-trips generally include a stop for a swim and lunch, sometimes on a deserted beach accessible only from the sea.

CHILDREN

The beaches of the Algarve, with long, sandy, gently shelving beaches for small children and small rocky coves ideal for older children to explore, are perfect for family holidays. Do pay attention to the beach warning flags, however. Green means the sea is calm and a life-guard is on duty; green plus a chequered flag means that no life-guard is on duty; yellow urges caution; red means danger and warns bathers to stay ashore.

The most popular choice for children off the beach is the nearest waterpark. The best are reckoned to be **Slide & Splash** (near Lagoa; see page 58) and **The Big One** (near Alcantarilha). **Atlantic Park** (Quatro Estradas, near Quarteira) has an attractive mountain backdrop and features a daily high-diving show. Its neighbour, **Aquashow,** has less in the way of aquathrills, but both children and adults get the chance to drive scaled-down Formula 1 cars on a mini racing circuit (Dad will need his driving licence).

Mini-Grand Prix cars are also an attraction close by at **Parcolandia,** but the main show here is a rather incongruous Hollywood-style recreation of the American Wild West with song-and-dance routines performed twice daily. There are also themed amusement park rides. Another attraction is Zoo-Marine, a small amusement park with performing dolphins and sea lions, a parrot show, a mini-zoo, a cinema, various children's fairground rides, and swimming pools.

BULLFIGHTS

The term "bullfight" is inaccurate in this instance, for this is no fight, but a ritual, which always has the same outcome. The big difference between the Portuguese and the Spanish corrida, however, is that in Portugal the bull leaves the ring bloodied but alive. Here it is not death in the afternoon, but the following morning in the slaughterhouse. The Portuguese version is further sanitized in that the bull's horns are blunted in order to reduce the risk of damage (to men and horses) by goring.

If you enjoy the colour, spectacle, and strategy of the bullfight but would prefer not to see the coup de grâce, then the Portuguese version may suit you. Be aware, though, that there is still plenty of blood. Like the Spanish version, the bull is used as a pincushion for long darts, then taunted and run to ground. Bullfights are held most Saturdays at Lagos, Albufeira, Quarteira, and Vila Real de Santo António.

NIGHTLIFE

The after-dark scene along the Algarve is generally cheap, cheerful, and unsophisticated. Resorts such as Albufeira and

Praia da Rocha throb to the disco beat and resound with karaoke, while visitors in the newer resorts may have to rely on their hotel for entertainment. Lagos (see page 63) is one of the few resorts with quiet night-time bars.

A flutist plays a tune in a folklore show.

Casinos operate at Praia da Rocha, Vilamoura, and Monte Gordo. They have restaurants with Las Vegas-style floor shows (open to all the family), and gambling takes place in a separate gaming room from mid-afternoon to well into the following morning. You must be 21 or over to gamble and will need your passport. Dress need not be formal but must be reasonably smart. Games on offer are roulette, blackjack, baccarat, and the Portuguese game of "French bank."

Another popular attraction is the *fado* night, at which distinctive Portuguese folk music is performed. There are two kinds of *fado*. The first and best known is the melancholy, nostalgia-tinged variety. Its origins are unclear. It may have developed as a mourning for men lost at sea or it may be a relic of the days of slavery—a kind of Iberian blues. The second kind is happy and upbeat, and, while lacking the emotional power of the former, at least gives the audience a chance to wring out their handkerchiefs. Typically the *fado* troupe will consist of a woman dressed in black accompanied by a couple of men playing acoustic guitars.

Festivals and Folklore

By comparison with the flamboyant fiestas of neighbouring Spain, Portugal's festivals are low-key. But each and every town does celebrate at least once a year on its saint's day, so check at the tourist information office when you arrive for forthcoming events (a monthly events leaflet is available). At any *festa* there is likely to be a solemn religious procession, majorettes (American-style), firemen holding polished ceremonial axes, and always fire-works. The best of these is the Carnival at Loulé, when spectacular flower-covered floats take to the street. Another lively spring festival is held in Alte on 1 May.

During May and June the Algarve Music Festival comprises free classical concerts by local and international musicians, plus other performing arts, in some of the region's oldest churches. September brings the National Folklore Festival and in October there are two major fairs: The Feira de Outubro at Monchique is famous for its market, while the Feira de Santa Iria at Faro is a lively traditional event lasting several days.

If you don't get to see folk dancing at any of these fairs, don't worry, as folklore shows are regularly staged in large resort hotels. Girls wear black felt hats over bright scarves, with colourful blouses and aprons over skirts with hoops. High-button shoes go over white knit stockings. In the swift whirling dances you'll notice the traditional long underwear, worn in spite of the climate. The men are dressed more soberly, with trousers, waistcoats, cummerbunds, and felt hats, mostly in black. Singers are accompanied by accordions, mouth organs, and triangles. There are basically two kinds of dances: the *coridinho*, or jig, whirlwind fast with stamping feet, and the *bailes de roda*, which are reels or square dances.

The Pequena Fonte restaurant in Alte hosts a lively folklore evening most nights and is a popular good-value excursion from far and wide. Look in local magazines for details of folklore events.

EATING OUT

Most Algarve cooking is as unaffected as a fisherman's barbecue: grilled or fried fish, chicken, steaks, and chops. If you want fancy French sauces, you'll have to find a fancy French restaurant. Which is not to say the Portuguese are not inventive. Who would have thought that combining clams and pork would make such a wonderful dish, or for that matter sole and bananas, or pork and figs.

You'll also find the spicy taste of Portugal's former colonies has crept into the national cuisine. Chicken piri-piri (made from Angolan peppers) is an ethnic-inspired dish and very popular in the Algarve. Curries occasionally appear on the menu, originating from the former colony of Goa (in Southern India) or Africa.

Prato do dia (dish of the day) often offers you a good meal at a fair price.

Fish and seafood is unfortunately no longer cheap, as much of it is brought from distant waters and catches are becoming less economical. The humble sardine is an exception, and with a hunk of peasant bread and a bottle of house wine you can still feast well on a small budget.

Meal Times

Breakfast (*o pequeno almoço*) and lunch (*o almoço*) are served at the usual European meal times. Dinner (*o jantar*) tends to be earlier than across the border in Spain, from about 7:30 to 9:30 P.M.

Breakfast

The Portuguese eat a light breakfast of coffee, toast or rolls, butter and jam. Hotels provide cooked English or American breakfasts.

Starters

As soon as you sit down you will be served a pre-starter snack which usually consists of bread, butter, and a combination of olives, sardine paste, and cream cheese (this isn't complimentary and will be on your bill as a cover charge).

Hearty starters always include a choice of soups—some vegetable soups, thickened with potatoes, can be almost a meal in themselves. Fish soup is variable but the Portuguese version of the cold Andalusian gazpacho (gaspacho) is usually good.

Casas de fagos or _adegas típicas_ are restaurants where you eat or drink to the sound of the _fado._

Fans of smoked food have two treats to look out for. The first is smoked ham (presunto fumado)—the best coming from Chaves, the northernmost province of Portugal (although Monchique ham is also highly regarded). The second is smoked swordfish (espadarte fumado), which is a little like smoked salmon but has a grainier texture and is less sweet. Most restaurants also have a range of international starters.

Fish and seafood

Prawns, crabs, lobsters, and fresh fish are always their own best advertisement, and you will see them all over the Algarve either refrigerated in a window display. or, in the case of large shellfish, swimming in an aquarium waiting for your selection. Most shellfish and some fish are sold on a price per kg basis.

Beware that if you choose lobster, it will probably be brought to your table alive and very much kicking, for your seal of approval. Fish priced on a weight basis will also be brought out to you (though not alive). Unless you are lucky enough to be on an expense account, this is when you must ask the exact cost. Large shellfish can be very expensive, so make sure you get a proper answer to avoid problems when the bill arrives. There are two kinds of lobster: a *lavagante* (with large front claws), and the *lagostim* or *lagosta* (the spiny lobster or crayfish, without claws). Similarly, there are two kinds of crab; the *sapateira* is a big Atlantic type, the *santola* is a spider crab.

Look out for the following seafood dishes:

Açorda de Marisco: a spicy, garlic-flavoured bread and seafood soup baked in a casserole, with raw eggs folded into the mixture at the table (also served as a starter).

Amêijoas à bulhão pato: clams, fried or steamed with garlic and coriander.

Arroz de Marisco: a seafood risotto.

Fresh, juicy prawns are just one ingredient of the feast of seafood offered in the Algarve.

All types of fresh fish are available in the Algarve.

Bacalhau: the cod that Portuguese have been drying and salting ever since their first sea voyages to Newfoundland in 1501. Strangely, even though fresh fish is available on their own doorstep, they still prefer to ship in this expensive, preserved fish, and it has become a national favourite. Preserving gives it a fuller flavour (though this is not always apparent when it is casseroled with many other ingredients). There are dozens of recipes for *bacalhau,* the most common on the Algarve being *à brás*—the cod is fried with onions and potatoes, then baked with a topping of beaten eggs.

Bife de Atum: a beefy fillet of tunny (tuna) steak, marinated in wine or vinegar, salt, garlic and bay leaves, then cooked with onion and perhaps bacon.

Caldeirada de peixe: the Algarve version of the French bouillabaisse, a rich, filling fish stew including potatoes, onions, tomatoes, pimentos, wine, and spices.

Cataplana: the region's most individual dish, named after the wok-like, primitive pressure-cooker in which it arrives. You may encounter several versions of the dish, but it is basically a combination of seafood, which always includes clams (*amêijoas*), plus salami-style sausage, ham, onion, garlic, paprika, a little chilli, parsley, and white wine. Don't go home without trying it.

Espadarte: swordfish, often grilled in a steak. On some menus it's listed as *peixe agulha.* Don't confuse it with *peixe espada*, a long thin fish, often translated as "scabbard fish."

Sardinhas: the best-value fish dish you'll enjoy on the Algarve; plump, juicy, crisply grilled, and served with boiled potatoes. Note that fresh sardines are only available from June to October, though at Portimão you will get them all year round (see page 59).

Meat and Fowl

Cabrito assado (no forno): Baked kid, not a common dish, but worth seeking out. *Cabrito estufado* is kid stewed with tomatoes and vegetables.

Carne de porco com amêijoas: an improbable but excellent combination of clams and pork, probably invented in the Alentejo, but since adopted by the Algarve.

Feijoada: a hearty dish consisting of dried beans and cabbage stewed with pork, sausage, bacon, and whatever else of the pig is to hand (often trotters).

Frango piri-piri: piri-piri are tiny red chilli peppers from Angola (you'll see them strung necklace-fashion in the market). They also appear in other dishes, but this one, barbecued chicken basted with a mix of chilli oil and vinegar, is probably the most popular meal on the Algarve.

Leito: roast suckling pig, served hot or cold.

Bife/Steak à Portuguêsa: steak fried with garlic, topped with ham, a fried egg, and served in a casserole dish surrounded by sautéed potatoes.

Dessert

The most prominent ingredients of Algarve desserts and confectionery are almonds, figs, and eggs. You'll need an extra sweet tooth to cope with some of them.

Arroz doce: rice pudding topped with cinnamon.

Pudim flan: a delicious crème caramel.

Pudim Molotov: an appropriately named tooth-melting, calorific bomb of fluffy egg-white mousse immersed in caramel sauce.

Tarte de amêndoa: almond tart.

Or you may prefer Portuguese cheese (*queijo*). The richest is *Serra da Estrela,* cured ewe's milk cheese from the country's highest mountain range. It takes some three hours to make each small cheese by hand and it is only available from December to April. Outside of this you'll have to make do with *Tipo Serra*, a harder, factory-made cheese. Other cheeses on offer include *Flamengo* (similar to Edam) and *Saloio*, a creamy type of cottage cheese.

Table Wines

Expensive restaurants aside, unless you specifically ask for the wine list, the waiter will simply ask you *tinto* (red) or *branco* (white). Of course you may want to extend your colour selection to rosé or *vinho verde* (green wine). The latter is named after its youth, not its colour, and has a slight but pleasant fizz. It goes particularly well with simple seafood dishes.

***à sua saude!* (ah sooer serooder) – cheers, literally "to your health"**

Of the local wines, you are most likely to see the Lagoa label, which packs more of a punch than average wine. The other principal Algarve area of wine production is Tavira.

Other Alcoholic Drinks

Port and Madeira have an image of being sweet and heavy and drunk only by retired colonels as digestifs. But both come in before- as well as after-dinner varieties, and it's well worth trying a glass of Sercial (dry Madeira). Verdelho (medium-dry Madeira) or a (dry) white Port. Two local wines that make excellent aperitifs are Algar Seco and Afonso III. Both come from Lagoa and are reminiscent of Sherry. Serve chilled.

After dinner try the totally breathtaking *medronho,* distilled from the fruit of the arbutus tree, or the equally powerful *bagaço,* or *bagaceira.* This firewater is made from grape residue in the same way as the French make *marc* and the

Don't Pass on the Port

Portugal's most famous drink is of course Port, though you would never know it from observing the average Algarve bar or restaurant. But if you ask a good barman or waiter, they will be delighted that you are taking an interest.

There are many different styles, but start off with a dry white Port. This is rather a misnomer as it resembles a delicious, full-bodied, medium-dry Sherry and makes an ideal aperitif.

Next try a "tawny" Port. The name refers to its colour—a light brown, and an Old Tawny will have a rich, nutty flavour.

Vintage Port is best of all, with a wonderful full, fruity taste. Strict rules apply to its production and bottling. A lot cheaper, but not necessarily less enjoyable, is Late Bottled Vintage Port.

Surprisingly there is only one Port cave in the whole of the Algarve—the Cave do Vinho do Porto in Albufeira. It's a good place to get started on your Port education.

Italians make *grappa*. *Brandymel* is an altogether gentler, sweeter taste, combining brandy and honey. If you want to sample a good local brandy, try the *Maceira* brand.

Coffee and tea

Most Portuguese order a *bica* when they want a coffee, which is a small expresso. If that's too small for you, order a *duplo,* which doubles the quantity. Take one *bica*, add water, and you have a *carioca*; a few drops of milk transforms it into a *garoto*.

If you are in a café and want a white coffee, ask for a *galão*, which is served in a tall glass. In a restaurant you would order a *café com leite*. There's no need to feel foreign when ordering tea (*chá*) since it has been drunk in Portugal as long as it has been known to the western world.

To Help You Order...

Could we have a table? **Queríamos uma mesa?**
I'd like a/an/some … **Queria** …

beer	**uma cerveja**	fish	**peixe**
mineral water	**água mineral**	rice	**arroz**
(sparkling)	**com gás**	fruit	**fruta**
(still)	**sem gás**	salad	**uma salada**
bill	**a conta**	ice-cream	um **gelado**
bread	**pão**	salt	**sal**
butter	**manteiga**	meat	**carne**
napkin	**um guarda-napo**	sandwich	**uma sanduíche**
		menu	**a ementa**
coffee	**um café**	soup	**uma sopa**
pepper	**pimenta**	milk	**leite**
dessert	**uma sobre-mesa**	sugar	**açúcar**
		tea	**um chá**
potatoes	**batatas**	wine	**vinho**

...and Read the Menu

alho	garlic	**frito**	fried
amêijoas	baby clams	**grão de bico**	chick-pea
ananás	pineapple	**guisado**	stew
assado	roast	**laranja**	orange
atun	tunny/tuna	**legumes**	vegetables
azeitonas	olives	**leitão**	suckling pig
bacalhau	cod (salted)	**linguado**	sole
besugo	sea-bream	**lombo**	fillet
bife (vaca)	steak (beef)	**lulas**	squid
bolo	cake	**maçã**	apple
borrego	lamb	**mariscos**	shellfish
cabrito	kid	**melancia**	watermelon
camarões	shrimp	**mexilhões**	mussels
caranguejo	crab	**molho**	sauce
cavala	mackerel	**morangos**	strawberries
cebola	onion	**ostras**	oysters
chouriço	spicy sausage	**ovo**	egg
churrasco	grilled meat	**pargo**	bream
coelho	rabbit	**pescada**	hake
cogumelos	mushrooms	**pescadinha**	whiting
costeletas	chops	**pêssego**	peach
couve	cabbage	**porco**	pork
cozido	boiled	**presunto**	ham
dobrada	tripe	**queijo**	cheese
enguias, eiros	eels	**robalo**	bass
ervilhas	peas	**salmonete**	red mullet
estufado	stewed/braised	**salsichão**	large sausage
feijões	beans	**sardinhas**	sardines
figos	figs	**torrada**	toast
framboesas	raspberries	**uvas**	grapes
frango	chicken	**vitela**	veal

INDEX

HANDY TRAVEL TIPS

An A–Z Summary of Practical Information

Listed after most main entries is an appropriate Portuguese translation, usually in the singular. You'll find this vocabulary useful when asking for information or assistance.

ACCOMMODATION (See also CAMPING on page 104, YOUTH HOSTELS on page 127 and the list of hotels from pages 129-135)

Hotels in the Algarve are graded from 2-star to 5-star deluxe and are of a good general international quality. For a touristic village (such as Vale do Lobo or Quinto do Lago), villas and apartments are rated up to 3 stars, with a luxury classification on top. Below the rating of hotel are estalagems ("inns," though not necessarily of the rustic type), then residencias and pensão (bed and breakfast hotels). An estalagem is usually smaller and simpler than a hotel of the same category. The quality of residencias and pensão is very variable, so don't accept a room without inspecting it. If you only require comfortable, simple accommodation, these are much cheaper and provide a more personal service than a hotel.

State-run pousadas (similar to the Spanish paradores) are sometimes installed in historic buildings such as castles or convents, or they may be housed in modern buildings, where a peaceful or scenic location is the main attraction. There are two pousadas in the Algarve, and both are modern; one at Sagres, which has an historic annexe in the Fortaleza do Beliche, and one above the village of São Brás de Alportel, which enjoys a peaceful setting.

I'd like a single/double room.	**Queria um quarto simples/duplo.**
with bath/shower	**com banho/chuveiro**
What's the rate per night?	**Qual é o preço por noite?**

AIRPORT *(aeroporto)*

Faro International Airport, serving the Algarve, is 7 km (4 miles) by road from Faro, the regional capital. It's a 10-minute taxi ride to

Faro, and about half an hour to Albufeira. There's also a bus service to Faro. Porters and trolleys are available.

Arriving passengers have a choice of several car-hire firms maintaining service desks at the airport. Helpful staff at the airport tourist information office will assist you with finding accomodation and any other queries you may have. Elsewhere in this bright, new terminal is a post office, a bank which opens late for currency exchange, a restaurant and bar open 24 hours, a news-stand, a souvenir shop, and a duty-free shop.

Airport Information	tel. (089) 80 06 17
TAP Air Portugal information	tel. (089) 80 07 31
British Airways information	tel. (089) 81 84 76/80 07 70

Where can I get a taxi?	**Onde posso encontrar un taxi?**
Please take these bags.	**Leve-me a baggagem, por favor.**

C

CAMPING *(campismo)*

Many of the Algarve's 23 camping sites are within easy reach of a beach. They range from very cheap, basic grounds (third class) to vast recreational centres with restaurants, pools, and sports facilities. Sites belonging to clubs or the Portuguese Federation of Camping and Caravanning are open to holders of a Camping Carnet (apply to the International Federation of Camping and Caravanning). There are also a number of privates sites which can only be used by members of the respective owners' associations.

Camping on beaches, or indeed anywhere outside recognized sites, is illegal. Details on all Algarve campsites are available from tourist information offices, or by writing to:

Federaçcão Portuguesa de Campismo e Caravanismo, Avenida 5 de Outubro 15–3, Lisboa 1000; tel. (01) 52 33 08/52 27 15.

Is there a campsite near here?	**Há algum parque de campsimo por aqui perto?**

May we camp here?	**Podemos acampar aqui?**
We have a caravan (trailer).	**Temos uma roulotte.**

CAR HIRE *(carros de aluguer)*

Local car-hire firms compete with the major international organizations at Faro Airport and all principal resorts. Normally the prices are alike.

You must be at least 21 and have held a valid national (or international) driving licence for at least one year. You will need to present a recognized credit card or a large cash deposit when booking. Third-party insurance is always included in the basic charge, and CDW is normally included if you book in advance. When booking in the Algarve check whether you need extra cover on this.

Your general travel insurance policy will normally cover you in the event of personal accidents, so you should not need personal accident isurance (PAI), but do check your policy to be on the safe side. A tax is added to the total rental bill when booking locally.

Note that the standard hire agreement will not cover you for driving in Spain.

I'd like to hire a car.	**Queria alugar um carro.**
tomorrow	**para amanhã**
for one day/week	**por um dia/uma semana**

CLIMATE

The Algarve climate is generally warm all year round with extremes being rare. However, winter evenings can sometimes be very chilly, and hot periods in July and August may be stifling to those who prefer milder weather.

Air temperature	**J**	**F**	**M**	**A**	**M**	**J**	**J**	**A**	**S**	**O**	**N**	**D**
°C	12	12	14	15	18	21	23	24	22	18	15	13
°F	54	54	57	59	64	69	73	75	72	64	59	55
Sea temperature												
°C	15	16	17	18	19	21	21	20	19	18	16	14
°F	59	61	62	64	66	69	69	67	66	64	61	57

CLOTHING

Pack a pullover, even in summer, as the evenings can turn quite cool. Winters are mild with the occasional shower, so a light rainproof jacket may come in handy. It's cooler in the mountains and also in Lisbon, so dress warmer if you are taking these excursions.

There's little formality on the Algarve, although if you are patronizing a luxury hotel or restaurant, or the casino, a certain degree of dressing up will be appreciated.

Will I need a tie?	**É preciso gravata?**
Is it all right if I wear this?	**Vou bem assim?**

COMPLAINTS

As a first principle always try to sort out any difficulties immediately with the manager or proprietor of the establishment concerned. If this is not possible, ask for the complaints book (*livro de reclamações*), which all establishments who deal with tourists must carry by law. Your complaint is written in triplicate; you keep a copy, the establishment keeps a copy, and the third copy goes to the regional tourism office. The very action of asking for the *livro* may be enough to resolve the problem, as the tourism authorities are able to revoke or suspend the licences of any establishments involved in malpractice.

You should also inform the local tourist office of any complaints you may have, and in serious cases ask them to enlist the assistance of the local police.

CRIME

The Spanish epidemic of theft from hire cars has now crossed the border to the Algarve. As a general rule, never leave anything in your car, even if it is out of sight and locked in the boot (trunk). In rural areas the problem is far less acute, but in tourist resorts and particularly where cars are left unattended for a period of time (at beach car parks, beauty spots, etc.) the risk is high.

Burglaries of holiday apartments, though less common than car theft, also occur, so be on your guard as far as possible. Leave any jewellery or other valuable items in your room safe deposit box, or with the hotel reception.

You must report all thefts to the local police and obtain a copy of your statement to them for insurance purposes. To add insult to injury, the Albufeira police actually make a charge for this service, so if you have lost your money you will have to borrow 200 escudos before going to see them!

If you are going to Lisbon, beware that the city is infamous for its pickpockets, particularly on the metro. You are also advised not to walk in the Bairro Alto or Alfama areas at night unless in a group.

On a more cheerful note, crimes involving violence against tourists are very rare in the Algarve.

I want to report a theft. **Quero participar um roubo.**

CUSTOMS and ENTRY FORMALITIES *(alfândega)*

Most visitors, including citizens of all EU countries, the U.S.A., Canada, Eire, Australia, and New Zealand need only a valid passport (no visa) to enter Portugal for 90 days (60 for U.S. citizens). The Portuguese-Spanish border scarcely serves as frontier anymore and visitors can come and go easily, though you should carry your passport.

Currency restrictions. Sums in excess of 1 million escudos in value must be declared on entry, and you cannot take out of the country more foreign currency than you brought in. You may not export more than 100,000 escudos in local currency, per person per trip.

Customs. There is no limit on the amount of goods that can be brought into Portugal from another EU country, but strict limits apply to the amount of duty-free goods that can be imported from outside the EU. The allowances are as follows: 200 cigarettes or 50 cigars or 250g tobacco; 1 litre of spirits (liquor), or 2 litres of liqueurs or fortified wines below 22% alcohol, or 2 litres of sparkling wine; and 2 litres of table wine.

Allowances for non-EU residents returning home are:

Into:	Cigarettes		Cigars		Tobacco	Spirits		Wine
Australia	200	or	250	or	250g	1 *l*	or	1 *l*
Canada	200	and	50	and	900g	1.1 *l*	or	1.1 *l*
New Zealand	200	or	50	or	250g	1.1 *l*	or	4.5 *l*
South Africa	400	and	50	and	250g	1 *l*	and	2 *l*
U.S.A.	200	and	100	or	*	1 *l*	and	1 *l*

*a reasonable amount

I've nothing to declare. **Não tenho nada a declarar.**

It's for my personal use. **É para uso pessoal.**

DRIVING

If you're driving all the way down to the Algarve, you need only your national driving licence, car registration papers, and the Green Card extension to your insurance—third party is obligatory, comprehensive is highly recommended. A warning triangle is also compulsory.

Driving conditions. The rules are the same as on the rest of the Continent: drive on the right, overtake on the left, yield right of way to all vehicles coming from your right. Speed limits are 120 km/h (74 mph) on motorways, 90 km/h (56 mph) outside built-up areas, and 60 km/h (37 mph) in built-up areas. The southern Algarve coastline is served by the Estrada Nacional (EN) 125. In places, this is a fast dual carriageway; from Lagos heading west, a new section has recently been completed. A few miles to the north, and running parallel to the EN 125, a new motorway has recently been completed, going from Spain as far west as Albufeira to adjoin the E01 Lisbon highway. The remainder of the roadway to Lagos is scheduled to be finished by the year 2000. It will divert traffic from the EN 125, which in summer can become a bumper-to-bumper nightmare. Be very careful, though, at all times on this road. Portuguese drivers are some of the worst in Europe and the accident rate is high.

Out of town you should also beware of such rustic hazards as herds of sheep or goats around the next bend, unlit donkeys and carts at night, tractors, haycarts, etc. If you intend driving to Lisbon allow at least 5 hours. The main road is surprisingly slow, and once you reach the centre of Lisbon traffic slows to a crawl.

Parking. Parking in most towns and resorts is manageable (although in Lisbon on-road parking is quite scarce). Don't be tempted to contravene any no-parking signs. Your car may be towed away. Sidelights are supposed to be left on in badly lit areas, and you should also park in the same direction as the flow of traffic.

Distances. Approximate road distances between Faro and principal towns:

	km	miles		km	miles
Albufeira	40	25	Sagres	110	68
Carvoeiro	60	37	Silves	55	34
Lagos	75	46	Tavira	30	18
Lisbon	300	186	Vila Real de Santo António	50	31
Portimão	60	37			

Rules and regulations. Front seat-belts are compulsory outside built-up areas. Children under 12 cannot sit in the front seat unless strapped into a special child restraint. New motoring laws brought in in the summer of 1993 mean you can be fined on the spot for not carrying your licence, passport, car-hire documents, for ignoring parking restrictions, and if you've drunk more than one glass of beer. Because of the risk of theft from your car, a photocopy of the important pages from your passport is more prudent and should suffice.

Breakdowns. There are SOS telephones stationed about every 3 km (2 miles) on main roads. If you belong to a motoring organization affiliated to the Automóvel Clube de Portugal (ACP) you can make use of their services free of charge. The emergency number for police and ambulance is 115 (free).

Road signs. Aside from the standard international pictographs you may encounter the following:

Alto	Halt
Bermas baixas	Keep off the verge (Soft shoulder)
Cruzamento	Crossroads
Curva perigosa	Dangerous bend (curve)
Descida ingreme	Steep hill
Desvio	Diversion (Detour)
Encruzilhada	Crossroads
Estacionamento permitido/ proibido	Parking permitted/no parking
Guiar com cuidado	Drive with care
Máquinas em manobras	Roadworks (men working)
Obras	Roadworks (men working)
Paragem (de autocarro)	Bus stop
Pare	Stop
Passagem proibida	No entry
Pedestres, peões	Pedestrians
Perigo	Danger
Posto de socorros	First-aid post
Proibida a entrada	No entry
Saída de camiões	Lorry (truck) exit
Seguir pela direita/esquerda	Keep right/left
Sem saída	No through road
Sentido proibido	No entry
Sentido único	One-way street
(Zona de) silêncio	Silence zone
Trabalhos	Roadworks (men working)
Trânsito proibido	No through traffic
Veículos pesados	Heavy vehicles
Velocidade máxima	Maximum speed

Can I park here? **Posso estacionar aqui?**

Are we on the right road for…?	**esta a estrada para…?**
Fill the tank, please with…	**Encha o depósito de…, por favor.**
Would you please change this tyre?	**Pode mudar o pneu, por favor?**
Check the oil/tyres/battery, please.	**Verifique o óleo/os pneus/a bateria, se faz favor.**
I've broken down.	**O meu carro está avariado.**
There's been an accident.	**Houve um acident.**

ELECTRIC CURRENT *(corrente eléctrica)*

The standard current is 220-volt, 50 cycle AC. Transformers and plug adapters are required for American appliances.

I need an adapter/a battery, please.	**Preciso de um adaptador/uma pilha, por favor.**

EMBASSIES and CONSULATES *(embaixada; consulado)*

A number of European countries have consuls or honorary consuls in the Algarve. For more serious matters, people are usually referred to their embassy in Lisbon.

British consulates: 7.1 Lg Francisco A Maurício, Portimão; tel. (082) 41 78 00; Rua General Humberto Delgado 4.

Embassies in Lisbon:

Canada: Avenida da Liberdade 144-156; tel. (01) 347-48-92.

Eire: Rua da Imprensa a Estrela 1; tel. (01) 66-15-69.

South Africa: Avenida Luís Bivar 10/10a; tel. (01) 53-50-41.

United Kingdom: Rua S. Domingos ã Lapa 37; tel. (01) 396-11-91.

USA: Avenida das Forças Armadas 16; tel. (01) 726-66-00.

Most embassies and consulates are open Monday to Friday, from 9 or 10am with a 1 to 2 hour lunch break.

EMERGENCIES *(urgência)*

The emergency number anywhere in Portugal is 115.

The hospitals at Faro and Portimão have *bancos de urgência* (emergency wards). Some hospitals can aso handle dental emergencies. For trouble on the road such as a breakdown, see DRIVING on page 108.

ETIQUETTE

The Portuguese are less outgoing on the whole than the Spanish, but in and around the tourist resorts they are certainly not shy. It's not too difficult to strike up a conversation, though generally you will have to make the first move.

Don't let it bother you if villagers off the beaten track seem to be staring at you; it's only unaffected curiosity. On the other hand it's often difficult to catch the eye of a waiter. The Portuguese have no equivalent for "Waiter!" but use the term *Faz favor* ("Please!").

How do you do?	**Muito prazer.**
How are you?	**Como está?**
Very well, thank you.	**Muito bem, obrigado/obrigada (f).**

G

GETTING TO THE ALGARVE

By Air

(See also AIRPORT on page 103) There are regular cheap charter flights to Faro from Britain and most major cities in Western Europe. Scheduled flights, operated by TAP Air Portugal and British Airways, are more expensive at the standard rate but can be competitive when on special offer. TAP and TWA fly from the USA, usually via Lisbon.

By Car

The main access road to Lisbon and the Algarve from France, through Spain, is at the western end of the Pyrenees. A motorway (expressway) runs from Biarritz (France) to Burgos. From there, take the N1 to Madrid and continue on the E4 via Badajoz and Setúbal, or the E4 to Mérida and then go via the E102 through Seville. As the distance from Calais to the Algarve is over 2,000 km (1,300 miles), you might like to consider the long-distance car ferry service from Plymouth to Santander in northern Spain (a 24-hour trip). From Santander follow the N611 and then the E3 via Valladolid and Coimbra.

By Rail

From Britain, cross the channel to and from there to Lisbon and Faro on the Sud Express; your ticket includes a ferry crossing across the River Tagus.

The InterRail Pass and InterRail 26+ Pass permit 15 or 30 days of unlimited rail travel in participating European countries. The Rail-Europe-Senior Card is available for senior citizens and entitles the holder to discount travel. Anyone living outside Europe or North Africa can purchase a Eurail-pass (before setting out) for unlimited rail travel in 16 countries, including Portugal (but not Britain).

GUIDES and TOURS

There are several guided day-trip itineraries available through hotels and travel agencies. These include Seville; Lisbon; the River Guadiana; Silves and Monchique; Sagres, Lagos, and the west; Loulé market and Alte; and a jeep safari. If you would like a personal guide to a particular place, the nearest tourist office or travel agency should be able to direct you to qualified local guides.

We'd like an English-speaking guide/an English interpreter.	**Queremos um guia que fa le inglês/um intérprete de inglês.**

LANGUAGE

A basic knowledge of Spanish will help you read signs and menus, but the spoken language is much more difficult to master. Almost all Portuguese understand Spanish, however, and in the tourist areas English is also widely spoken.

The *Berlitz Portuguese Phrasebook and Dictionary* covers most of the situations you're likely to encounter. Also useful is the *Berlitz*

Portuguese–English/English–Portuguese Pocket Dictionary, which contains a special menu-reader supplement.

There is a list of useful expressions on the inside front cover of this guide and also on page 128, but here are a few words to get you going:

Good morning	**Bom dia**
Good afternoon	**Boa tarde**
Good evening	**Boa noite**
Please	**Por favor**
Thank you	**Obrigado** (women say **obrigada)**
Goodbye	**Adeus**
Yes/No	**Sim/Não**
Do you speak English?	**Fala inglês?**
I don't understand.	**Não compreendo.**
I don't speak Portuguese.	**Não falo português.**
Where is the… consulate?	**Onde é o consulado…?**
American/British/Canadian	**americano/britânico/canadiano**

LOST PROPERTY *(objectos perdidos)*

Go to the nearest police station to report the loss and they will issue you with an official form which you must fill in for your own insurance purposes. There is no central office for lost property in the Algarve.

I've lost my…	**Perdi…**
wallet/bag/passport.	**a minha carteira/o meu saco/ o meu passaporte.**

M

MAPS

The Algarve is a relatively small region, interlinked from east to west by the EN 125, so orientation is easy. However, if you intend exploring the roads less travelled, then the Hildebrand *Travel Map to the Algarve* (1:100,000) is a good buy. All tourist information offices will supply you with a reasonable street plan of the local town.

a street map of…	**uma planta de…**
a road map of the Algarve	**um mapa das estradas do Algarve**

MEDICAL CARE (see also EMERGENCIES on page 112)

All the principal Algarve towns have hospitals; many have doctors who speak other languages. Tourist offices carry lists of doctors and dentists who speak English. Travel insurance to cover medical expenses is always sensible, and EU residents may also obtain form E111 before departure. This entitles you to free medical treatment while on holiday in the Algarve. If you don't have your E111 with you, you'll have to pay up on the spot and claim it back on your travel insurance policy.

Common ailments include sunburn, through too much exposure too soon (take it easy for the first few days and never fall asleep in the sun), and hangovers from an excess of alcohol, not helped by the devil-may-care spirit measure served in these parts. Mosquitoes are around in summer, so an anti-mosquito device which simply plugs into your wall and emits a vapour that is noxious to the insect, but not to you, is very worthwhile (available at airport shops).

Chemists (*farmácias*) are recognizable by a green cross sign and open during normal shop hours. After hours, one pharmacy in town takes it in turns to open late and its name and location is posted in the window of the other *farmácias*.

Where's the nearest (all night) pharmacy?	**Onde fica a farmácia (de serviço) mais próxima?**
I need a doctor/dentist.	**Preciso de um médico/dentista.**
I'm not feeling well.	**Não me sinto bem**
I've got a fever.	**Tenho febre.**
I have toothache.	**Tenho dor de dentes.**
an ambulance	**uma ambulância**
hospital	**hospital**
sunburn	**queimadura de sol**
sunstroke	**uma insolação**
a fever	**febre**

an upset stomach	**uma indigestão**
insect bite	**uma picadela de insecto**

MONEY MATTERS (For currency restrictions, see CUSTOMS AND ENTRY FORMALITIES on page 107)

Currency. Don't be worried when you see price tags with the $ sign. Here it means *escudo* (abbreviated esc), and the sign often replaces the decimal point, so 50$00 means 50 escudos. The escudo is divided into 100 *centavos*, but you don't see these any more. Coins in use are 1, 21/2, 5, 10, 20, 50, 100, and 200 escudos. Banknotes come in denominations of 500, 1,000 (one *conto*), 2,000, 5,000, and 10,000 escudos.

Banking hours are generally from 8:30am to 3pm Monday to Friday. During the height of the tourist season, at least one bank in the bigger towns and resorts stays open after hours and on Saturdays. The exchange office at Faro Airport stays open until the last major flight of the evening. Changing money can be quite expensive, and you are advised to check the rate of commission before any transaction. Banks levy a minimum charge of 500–1,000 escudos for traveller's cheques, so it is not a good idea to exchange small amounts with them. Use either your hotel or a bureau de change and shop around for the lowest rate.

Credit cards, traveller's cheques, Eurocheques. These are accepted in most establishments, although paying by cheque will invariably be more expensive than by cash, due to the establishment's lower rate of exchange.

Where's the nearest bank/ currency exchange office?	**Onde fica o banco mais próximo/ a casa de câmbio mais próxima?**
I want to change some pounds/dollars.	**Queria trocar libras/dólares.**
Can I cash a traveller's cheque?	**Posso trocar um cheque de viagem?**

Can I pay with this credit card?	**Posso pagar com este cartão de crédito?**
How much is that?	**Quanto custa isto?**

PLANNING YOUR BUDGET

The following list will give you some idea of what to expect in the Algarve. Although the Algarve has experienced low inflation, please consider these as approximations.

Babysitters. 1,500 escudos per hour (2,000 escudos after midnight).

Beach. Two sunbeds and an umbrella/parasol 750 escudos per day.

Bicycle hire. 1,500–1,800 escudos per day.

Big-game fishing. 12,000 escudos per day (spectators 10,000 escudos).

Camping. From 900 escudos per person with tent; from 1,200 escudos per caravan/trailer.

Car hire. (average local and international companies) Group A *(Opel Corsa 1.0/Fiat Panda)* 1–3 days 4,000 escudos per day, 7 days 3,800 escudos per day. Group B *(Peugeot 205/Fiat Uno)* 1–3 days 5,000 escudos per day, 7 days 4,500 escudos per day. Group C *(Ford Fiesta/Renault Clio)* 1–3 days 6,000 escudos per day, 7 days 5,500 escudos per day.

Entertainment. Waterpark, adult 2,500 escudos, child 1,500 escudos; bullfight 2,000 escudos.

Excursions (day trips include lunch). Seville 8,000 escudos, Lisbon 8,500 escudos, River Guadiana boat trip 7,000 escudos, Monchique/Silves 6,000 escudos, Loulé/Alte (half day) 2,500 escudos, jeep safari 6,500 escudos.

Hotels. (double room with bath/shower per night) ***—high season 14,000 escudos, mid-season 8–12,000 escudos, low season 8,000 escudos. ****—high season 17–25,000 escudos, mid-season 15,000 escudos, low season 10,000 escudos. *****—high season 35,000+ escudos, mid-season 30,000 escudos, low season 18,000 escudos.

Meals and drinks. Continental breakfast (in hotel) 750 escudos; three-course meal for two including a bottle of wine in a reasonable establishment 5,000–8,000 escudos; tea/coffee 78–120 escudos; beer 100–150 escudos; soft drink 100–250 escudos.

Motorcycle hire. 2,000–4,000 escudos per day.

Nightlife. Cinema 700–1,000 escudos, disco from 1,500–2,000 escudos (includes first drink), casino entrance 2,000 escudos.

Petrol. 163 escudos per litre.

Food and drink. Small loaf bread 50 escudos, butter (250g) 300 escudos, instant coffee (100g) 250 escudos, orange juice (1 litre) 330 escudos, wine from 350 escudos per bottle.

Sports. *Golf* 6,000–12,500 escudos for green fees for an 18-hole championship course. Club and trolley hire around 3,500 escudos. *Horseback-riding* 2,500–3,500 escudos per hour. *Tennis* 1,000 escudos per court per hour. Equipment hire—racquets 400 escudos, balls 300 escudos. *Water-skiing* 5,000 escudos per session. *Jet-skiing* 2,000 escudos per 10 minutes. *Tuition* for most sports 5,000–6,000 escudos per hour.

Taxi. 200 escudos flat charge (includes first 700 metres) plus 56 escudos per km.

N

NEWSPAPERS and MAGAZINES *(jornal; revista)*

Europe's principal papers, including most British dailies and the *International Herald Tribune*, are on the news-stands the same day as publication. Popular foreign magazines and paperback books in English are also widely available.

English-language publications which include useful information as to what's on (folklore, markets, music, cinema, sporting events, etc.) include: *The Algarve News*, a fortnightly newspaper; and the *Algarve Resident*, a weekly magazine. The *Discover* series of monthly magazines, which also give information about forthcoming local events, are particularly useful, and can be picked up free at tourist offices.

Have you any English-language newspapers/magazines?	**Tem jornais/revistas em inglês?**

OPENING HOURS

The Portuguese do not take a siesta, but most businesses close for a 1–2 hour lunch break. The following are general times:

Banks: 8:30am to 3pm Monday-Friday (see MONEY MATTERS on page 116).

Bars and restaurants: In resorts many bars are open from noon (or earlier) until the small hours. Informal restaurants may open all day but smarter establishments may only open at lunch and in the evening. Some restaurants close one day a week, so it is a good idea to check first with the establishment (see RESTAURANTS on pages 136-143).

Markets: 8am–1pm

Post offices: Main offices 8:30 or 9am to 6:30 or 7pm Monday-Friday, local branches 9am to 12:30pm and 2 to 6pm Monday-Friday.

Shops: 9am to 1pm Monday-Saturday and 3 to 7pm Monday-Friday (closed Saturday afternoon and Sunday).

PHOTOGRAPHY

All the popular brands, types of film, and camera accessories are sold in the Algarve at competitive prices, and 24-hour processing is widely available.

Field workers, fishermen, and local people can make very photogenic subjects, but do have the courtesy to ask before you snap. Most do not mind and are sometimes amused, but you may well offend elderly people. Do remember you are a guest in their country.

Do not attempt to take photographs at airports, military docks, or anywhere that it could even remotely be construed that you were breaching security.

I'd like a film for this camera.	**Quero um rolo para esta máquina.**
a black-and-white film	**um rolo a preto e branco**
a colour film	**um rolo a cores**
35-mm film	**um rolo de trinta e cinco milímetros**
May I take a picture?	**Posso tirar uma fotografia?**

POLICE *(polícia)*

During the summer in those resorts and towns with tourist traffic, look for the police wearing armbands marked CD (it stands for Corpo Distrital, meaning local corps). They are assigned to assist tourists and normally speak a foreign language.

On highways, traffic is controlled by the Guarda Nacional Republicana (GNR) in white cars or on motorcycles. The correct way to address any policeman is Senhor Guarda.

Where's the nearest police station?	**Onde fica o posto de policia mais próximo?**

POST OFFICES *(correios)* (See also TELEPHONES on page 124)

Post offices are indicated by the letters CTT (*Correios, Telegrafos e Telefones*). The mail service is generally good, though it can get bogged down during the height of the season. You can buy stamps from most shops as well—they usually display a sign: *Correios*. Most mailboxes follow the British pillar-box design and are even painted bright red.

Main post office hours are 8:30 or 9am to 6:30 or 7pm Monday to Friday; local branches open 8:30am to 3pm (some close for lunch). The main post offices in Portimão and Faro open on Saturday mornings as well. Telegrams (*telegrama*) can be sent from post offices (but remember that in Britain this service no longer exists), or you can give the text to your hotel receptionist. Many hotels have telex facilities, and there are public telexes in main post offices.

Where's the nearest post office?	**Onde fica a estação eoffice?eios mais próxima?**
Have you received any mail for?	**Tem correio para…?**
A stamp for this letter/ postcard, please.	**Um selo para esta carta/este postal, por favor.**
express (special delivery)	**expresso**
airmail	**via aérea**
registered	**registado**
I want to send a telegram to…	**Quero mandar um telegrama para…**

Posta Restante (*general delivery*). If you don't know where you'll be staying, you can have mail sent posta restante to any post office convenient to you. For example: Mr John Smith, Posta Restante, 8200 Albufeira, Portugal. You'll need to produce your passport or identity card when collecting your mail.

PUBLIC HOLIDAYS *(feriado)*

1 Jan	*Ano Novo*	New Year's Day
25 April	*Dia da Liberdade*	Liberty Day
1 May	*Festa do Trabalho*	Labour Day
10 June	*Dia de Portugal*	National Day
15 Aug	*Assunção*	Assumption
5 Oct	*Heróis da República*	Republic Day
1 Nov	*Todos-os-Santos*	All Saints' Day
1 Dec	*Dia da Independência*	Independence Day
8 Dec	*Imaculada Conceição*	Immaculate Conception
25 Dec	*Natal*	Christmas Day

Movable dates:	*Carnaval*	Shrove Tuesday
	Sexta-feira Santa	Good Friday
	Corpo de Deus	Corpus Christi

These are only the national holidays of Portugal. Other special holidays may affect different places at other times. And every town closes down and takes to the streets at least once a year in honour of its own patron saint.

Are you open tomorrow? **Estão abertos amanhã?**

PUBLIC TRANSPORT

Buses *(autocarro).* Evas Transportes operates most buses in the Algarve. A few vehicles assigned to the remote local services are somewhat rickety, but most are modern and comfortable. A baffling variety of local and regional timetables may be consulted at any bus station or tourist information office. Perhaps surprisingly, most buses run on time. Buy your ticket on board the bus for all services except for the Algarve Express, where tickets must be purchased in advance at the station. Bus stops are denoted by the sign "Paragem."

Inter-city buses. Evas Transportes and some private firms run express coaches which link Algarve towns and resorts with Lisbon. Some have air-conditioning as well as other amenities. Travel agencies can provide full details.

Trains *(comboio).* A railway line runs from Lagos in the west to the eastern frontier at Vila Real de Santo António. Stations are in or near the main towns, but sometimes far enough away to require a bus or taxi ride. The most notable example is the station of Albufeira, which is actually near Ferreiras and a good 15-minute bus ride from the resort (the bus and train timetables are not synchronized). There is not a great deal of difference in time or price between long-distance buses and trains, but the latter do offer unspoiled scenery.

Many trains have first- and second-class carriages. A first-class coach is marked by a yellow stripe above the windows and a number "1" near the doors. There are no restaurant cars on Algarve trains.

A railway line links the Algarve with Lisbon. The fastest trains take just three hours to cover the distance between the Algarve junction Tunes, and Barreiro, across the River Tagus from Lisbon.

Where is the nearest railway station/bus stop?	**Onde é a estação ferroviária/ a paragem de autocarros maispróxima?**
When's the next bus/train to...?	**Quando parte o próximo autocarro/comboio para...?**
I want a ticket to...	**Queria um bilhete para...**
single (one-way trip)	**ida**
return (round-trip)	**ida e volta**
first/second class	**primeira/segunda classe**
Will you tell me when to get off?	**Pode dizer-me quando devo descer?**

R

RADIO and TV *(rádio; televisão)*

There are two government-operated TV channels in Portugal, and Spanish television is also received in the east. Most big hotels and many larger bars also have satellite TV showing feature films, football matches, and other big sporting events. For details pick up a copy of the Algarve Resident.

Tune into Solar Radio (90.5 fm) for English news bulletins at 8:30am and also later in the day, and Kiss FM (101.2 FM) for rock and pop music. You may well also be able to pick up Spanish and Moroccan programmes. The BBC World Service, Voice of America, and Radio Canada International can be heard on short wave.

RELIGION

The vast majority of Portuguese are Roman Catholic. Services in English are scheduled in principal tourist areas. Protestant (primarily Anglican) services are held in several towns; full details of all services are available from tourist offices and most hotels.

RESTAURANTS See EATING OUT on page 91 and RECOMMENDED RESTAURANTS starting on page 136. In addition to these, *pousadas* (see ACCOMMODATION on page 103) can be relied on for good local food.

TAXIS *(táxi)*

Portuguese taxis are black with green roofs or cream-coloured. Drivers are not allowed to pick up customers in the street so you will have to go to a taxi rank or telephone for a cab. The majority of taxis are metered. If your taxi doesn't have a meter, make sure you ask what the charge will be before setting out.

Where can I get a taxi?	**Onde posso encontrar um táxi?**
What's the fare to…?	**Quanto custa o percurso para…?**

TELEPHONES *(Telefone)*

Automatic coin and card telephones are found in bars and restaurants and on the street. To make an international call, buy a Credifone phonecard rather than fumbling with mountains of coins. These are on sale at several shops. The other alternative is to make your call from a post office, where you go to a booth and pay the person at the desk after the call. The cost of this is the same as a coin or card phone. Calls from your hotel will be at least double.

Dial 099 for the international operator for Europe, 098 for the rest of the world. For international direct dialling use 00, followed by the area code (without the first 0) then the number.

Telephone Spelling Code:

A	Aveiro	J	José	S	Setúbal
B	Braga	K	Kodak	T	Tavira
C	Coimbra	L	Lisboa	U	Unidade
D	Dafundo	M	Maria	V	Vidago
E	Évora	N	Nazaré	W	Waldemar
F	Faro	O	Ovar	X	Xavier
G	Guarda	P	Porto	Y	York

H	Horta	Q	Queluz	Z	Zulmira
I	Itália	R	Rossio		

Can you get me this number?	**Pode ligar-me para este número?**
reverse-charge (collect) call	**paga pelo destinatário**
person-to-person (personal) call	**com pré-aviso**

TIME DIFFERENCES

Algarve and the rest of Portugal are on Greenwich Mean Time year-round:

Summer time chart

Los Angeles	New York	London	**Algarve**	Madrid
3am	6am	11am	**11am**	noon

What time is it, please? **Que horas são, por favor?**

TIPPING

Hotel and restaurant bills are usually all-inclusive, so tipping is not obligatory. But if the service has been good you might like to give the following:

Hairdresser/Barber	10%
Hotel maid, per week	500 esc
Lavatory attendant	25 esc
Hotel porter, per bag	50 esc
Taxi driver	10%
Tour guide	10–15% of excursion fare
Waiter	10-15% of bill

TOILETS *(casa de banho)*

The best place to find a clean toilet is a large hotel. You can also use bar or restaurant facilities, but out of courtesy you should buy a drink. The Ladies' is marked Senhoras and the Gents' Homens.

Where are the toilets? **Onde são as casas de banho?**

TOURIST INFORMATION OFFICES *(turismo)*

Information on the Algarve may be obtained from the Portuguese National Tourist Office in many countries, including:

Canada: Suite 1005, 60 Bloor Street West, Toronto, Ontario M4W 3B0; tel. (416) 921-7376.

Great Britain: 22/25a Sackville Street, London W1X 1DE; tel. (0171) 494 1441.

U.S.A.: 4th Floor, 590 Fifth Avenue, New York NY 10036; tel. (212) 354 4403.

In the Algarve itself, all the major (and some minor) towns have tourist information offices, staffed by helpful English-speaking assistants. Always make the turismo your first stop and pick up the town map/brochure (printed in several languages), which locates all major points of interest.

TRAVELLERS WITH DISABILITIES

Both Faro and Lisbon airports are accessible to wheelchair users. Public transport, however, is mostly of the aged variety and therefore not very wheelchair-friendly. IHD International (Marconistraat 3, 6716 AK Ede, The Netherlands) offer a wheelchair-accessible bus between Faro Airport and Albufeira and Vilamoura, and can also provide a support package for disabled people who are on holiday in the Algarve.

The National Rehabilitation Secretariat, Avenida Conde Valbom 63, 1000 Lisbon, publishes a guide to transport facilities (in Portuguese only) and an Access Guide to Lisbon with symbols explained in English. The Portuguese National Tourist Office can provide a list of hotels with few barriers to wheelchair users; a list of accessible Algarve hotels and campsites is also given in Holidays and Travel Abroad, published by RADAR, 12 City forum, 250 City Road, London EC1V 8AF; tel. (0171) 250 3222. See also the list of recommended hotels in this guide from pages 129-135. If you need to hire a wheelchair while in the Algarve, go to the nearest Nursing Centre (Centros de Enfermagem).

Finally, before you go, contact the Holiday Care Service, who are experts in the field of holidays for disabled people and will try to answer specific queries; tel. (01293) 774535.

W

WATER *(água)*

Since tap water is not universally safe to drink, you are advised to stick to bottled mineral water—this is sold cheaply everywhere, usually under the Monchique label.

a bottle of mineral water	**uma garrafa de água mineral**
sparkling (carbonated)/still	**com/sem gás**

Y

YOUTH HOSTELS *(pousadas de juventude)*

There are four youth hostels in the Algarve, at Portimão, Lugar da Coca Maravilhas (tel. 85–704); at Vila Real de Santo António, Rua Dr Sousa Martins (tel. 44–565); at Alcoutim (tel. 81-460-04); and at Lagos (tel. 82-761-760). Young tourists, from 14 up, can stay in dormitories at very low rates if they're members of a national or international youth hostel organization. Family rooms are also available. Portuguese membership is open to "juniors" (aged 14–21) and seniors (22–45). Don't worry too much if any of your party is outside the age bracket, it is a preference, not a hard-and-fast rule.

The headquarters of the Portuguese Youth Hostel Association (Associação Portuguesa de Pousadas de Juventude) is at: 137 Avenida Duque Avila, 1050 Lisbon; tel. (13) 55-90-81.

Is there a youth hostel near here?	**Há alguma pousada de juventude aqui perto?**

SOME USEFUL EXPRESSIONS

(See also the inside front cover of this guide and LANGUAGE on page 113 for some further useful expressions)

excuse me/you're welcome	**perdão/de nada**
where/when/how?	**onde/quando/como?**
how long/how far?	**quanto tempo/a que distância?**
yesterday/today/tomorrow	**ontem/hoje/amanhã**
day/week/month/year	**dia/semana/mês/ano**
left/right	**esquerdo/direito**
good/bad	**bom/mau**
big/small	**grande/pequeno**
cheap/expensive	**barato/caro**
hot/cold	**quente/frio**
old/new	**velho/novo**
open/closed	**aberto/fechado**
up/down	**em cima/em baixo**
here/there	**aqui/ali**
free (vacant)/occupied	**livre/ocupado**
early/late	**cedo/tarde**
easy/difficult	**fácil/difícil**
Please write it down.	**Escreva-mo, por favor.**
Is there an admission charge?	**Paga-se entrada?**
Have you something less expensive?	**Tem qualquer coisa de mais barato?**
Just a minute.	**Um momento.**
Get a doctor, quickly!	**Chame um médico, depressa!**

Recommended Hotels

Below is a selection of hotels in different price bands covering the major towns and resorts of the Algarve. Book well in advance for the high season. This particularly applies for smaller establishments.

"Disabled access" denotes that the hotel claims to be accessible to disabled guests, or that there are few obstacles to wheel-chairs. Try to confirm your requirements in advance.

The star rating in brackets after each hotel name refers to the official government grading system (see ACCOMMODATION on page 103). As a basic guide to room prices we have used the following symbols (for a double room with bath/shower in high season):

✪	below 10,000 esc
✪✪	10,000–16,000 esc
✪✪✪	17,000–25,000 esc
✪✪✪✪	above 25,000 esc

ALBUFEIRA

Cerro Alagoa (****) ✪✪✪ *Tel. 58 02 10 00, Fax 58 02 199.* One of Albufeira's newest and most stylish 4-star hotels, this lively establishment offers an English bar, a jungle-themed swimming pool, sauna, and gymnasium. 310 rooms.

Hotel da Aldeia (****) ✪✪✪ *Areias de São João, (2 km/1.2 miles from Albufeira), Tel. 58 88 61, Fax 58 88 64.* Modern 5-storey hotel with large terraces overlooking gardens, two swimming pools, a tennis court, and a mini-golf course. Disabled access. 128 rooms.

Bellavista Avenida Apartments (****) ✪✪✪ *Quinta da Bellavista, Tel. 58 71 31, Fax 58 69 77.* Beautifully furnished apartments in the new part of town. Two swimming pools, children's play-area.

Hotel Boa Vista (****) ✪✪✪ *Rua Samora Barros 20, Tel. 58 91 75, Fax 58 91 80.* Superb setting, built into the cliff at the very western end of town, with a view over the whole of Albufeira. Close enough to walk to town but far enough away to be quiet in high season. Swimming pool and sun terrace. 93 rooms.

Hotel California (***) ✪✪✪ *Rua Cândido dos Reis 10–16, Tel. 58 68 33, Fax 58 68 50.* In the very middle of town, on the hillside. Old-fashioned decor and pleasant, friendly staff. Rooftop swimming pool and sauna. 56 rooms.

Estalagem do Cerro (****) ✪✪–✪✪✪ *Rua Cerro da Piedade, Tel. 58 61 91, Fax 58 61 94.* Enjoying a similar location to Hotel Boa Vista, this modern 4-storey establishment has the comforts of a 4-star hotel at 3-star prices. Outdoor pool and garden, health club with gym, sauna, solarium, and jacuzzi. 83 rooms.

Hotel Montechoro (****) ✪✪✪ *Montechoro (3.5 km/2 miles from Albufeira), Tel. 58 94 32, Fax 58 99 47.* This modern hotel has extensive grounds, well-equipped rooms, excellent restaurants, waterpark, swimming pools, eight tennis courts, squash, sauna, and gym. Disabled access. 362 rooms.

Vila Magna Albufeira Jardim Apartments (****) ✪✪ *Cêrro da Piedade, Tel. 58 69 72, Fax 58 69 77.* To the west of the town centre, these well-equipped apartments enjoy fine views. Quiet setting, only 5 minutes' walk into town. Attractive swimming pool area, indoor pool, tennis courts, disco, and games facilities. 470 apartments.

Hotel Rocamar (***) ✪✪–✪✪✪ *Largo Jacinto d'Ayet, Tel. 58 69 90, Fax 58 69 98.* A modern, 7-storey hotel in an enviable position nestled into the cliff-face looking onto the main town beach. 91 rooms.

Residencial Villa Recife (***) ✪✪ *Rua Miguel Bombarda 6, Tel. 58 67 47.* Two minutes' walk from the town centre, this is a converted private house in a pretty garden. If you're after character accommodation, request a room in the old part of the house, rather than the modern wing. 92 rooms.

Hotel Baltum (**) ✪✪ *Avenida 25 de Abril, Tel. 58 91 02, Fax 58 61 46.* Cheap, cheerful hotel accommodation for those wishing to stay in the town centre, popular with the young. Terrace restaurant/bar plus solarium. Free use of Hotel California facilities (see above). 53 rooms.

ALVOR

Hotel Delfim (****) ✪✪✪–✪✪✪✪ *Praia dos Três Irmãos (2 km/1.2 miles from Alvor), Tel. 45 89 01, Fax 45 89 70.* Set 200 metres (215 yards) from the beach, this large, modern luxury hotel offers an impressive seawater swimming pool (with bar set in the middle), seven tennis courts, and a health club. Rooms are large and well equipped. 325 rooms.

Hotel Dom João II (****) ✪✪✪–✪✪✪✪ *Praia de Alvor, (1 km/0.6 miles from Alvor), Tel. 45 91 35, Fax 45 93 63.* Part of the Torralta holiday complex, this 7-storey hotel is bright and airy with a large swimming pool and spacious sun terraces. The Torralta complex offers a wide range of sporting facilities. 219 rooms.

FARO

Hotel Eva (****) ✪✪✪ *Avenida da República, 1, Tel. 80 33 54, Fax 80 23 04.* The best hotel in Faro, recently refurbished. A large, modern block on the edge of the harbour 91 metres (100 yards) from the shops and the old town. Several bars and restaurants, a disco, and folklore shows. 150 rooms.

Pensão Casa de Lumena (***) ✪ *Praça Alexandre Herculano 27, Tel. 80 19 90, Fax 80 40 19.* This 150-year-old building, located in the centre of Faro, is a town-house conversion and still retains much of its character. 12 rooms.

Pensão O'Farão (***) ✪ *Largo da Madalena 4, Tel. 82 33 56.* Don't be put off by the frontage or the rather shabby square on which this little gem stands. Inside are gleaming *azulejos* and fine traditional decor and furnishing. Breakfast on the roof terrace. Good central location, friendly owners, excellent value. 13 rooms.

Residencial Afonso III (***) ✪ *Rua Miguel Bombarda 64, Tel. 80 35 42, Fax 80 51 85.* Simple, clean, and pleasant hotel in the centre of Faro. Bar. 43 rooms.

LAGOS

Penina Golf & Resort Hotel (*****) ✪✪✪✪ *On route EN 125, between Lagos and Portimão, Tel. 41 54 15, Fax 41 50 00.* One of the Algarve's finest luxury hotels, set within a 146-hectare (360-acre) estate, which includes the world-famous Penina golf course. Perfect for the well-heeled sports lover with Penina green fees, floodlit tennis, sailing, windsurfing, and circuit training all included in room rate. 192 rooms.

Hotel Golfinho (****) ✪✪✪ *Praia Dona Ana, Tel. 76 99 00, Fax 76 99 99.* Perfectly placed above the picturesque beach of Dona Ana, this modern 8-storey block has indoor and outdoor swimming pools, a bowling alley, and disco. Disabled access. 270 rooms.

Hotel de Lagos (****) ✪✪✪ *Rua Nova da Aldeia, Tel. 76 99 67, Fax 76 99 20.* Large modern hotel near Old Town. Attractive poolside areas, indoor swimming pool, jacuzzi, fitness centre, tennis courts, plus watersports at the Duna Beach Club. 318 rooms.

Hotel Meia Praia (***) ✪✪✪ *Meia Praia, Tel. 76 20 01, Fax 76 20 08.* A 3-storey block situated on the beach of Meia Praia, 3 km (2 miles) from town. Two swimming pools, two tennis courts, mini-golf, and landscaped gardens. Disabled access. 66 rooms.

Hotel Rio Mar (***) ✪✪ *Rua Cândido dos Reis 83, Tel. 76 30 91, Fax 76 39 27.* Functional modern block, notable more for its town centre location than quality of accommodation. Sunbathing terrace. 42 rooms.

Hotel São Cristovão (***) ✪✪ *Avenida dos Descobrimentos, Tel. 76 30 51, Fax 45 91 71.* Modern, white block just outside the town centre. Guests may use the pool at the Hotel Meia Praia (see above) to which a complimentary bus runs. 80 rooms.

Residencial Casa de São Gonçalo de Lagos (****) ✪✪ *Rua Cândido dos Reis 73, Tel. 76 21 71, Fax 76 39 27.* This fine old mansion in the heart of town dates back to the 18th century. Stone staircases lead to rooms and landings filled with antiques, and there is a lovely patio and lounge. 13 rooms.

Residencial Lagosmar (***) ✪ *Rua Dr Faria Silva 13, Tel. 76 35 23, Fax 76 37 24.* Tucked away in a sidestreet off the main square of Praça Gil Eanes, this small, spotless town-house conversion provides excellent value accommodation. The roof-terrace with panoramic views is a bonus. 45 rooms.

OLHOS DE AGUA

Sheraton Algarve (Pine Cliffs) Hotel & Resort (*****) ✪✪✪✪ *Praia da Falésia, Tel. 50 19 99; Fax 50 19 50.* One of the Algarve's newest and most luxurious developments, surrounded by pines at the top of dramatic cliffs. Spectacular Moorish styling, excellent restaurants, extensive sporting facilities including a 9-hole golf course with its own resident professional, tennis, private beach, watersports, and yachting. 215 rooms.

Alfa Mar (****) ✪✪✪ *Praia da Falésia, Tel. 50 13 51, Fax 50 14 04.* Large, modern building located on a grassy clifftop high above the beach. An excellent choice for sports enthusiasts with its several tennis courts, a health club, watersports, and athletics facilities. 264 rooms.

Hotel Falesia (***) ✪✪✪ *Sitio do Roja Pé, Tel. 50 12 37, Fax 50 12 70.* Modern hotel with good service, situated next to the Sheraton. All rooms have en suite bathrooms, satellite TV, private safe. Large parking area, pool. 145 rooms.

PRAIA DA ROCHA

Hotel Algarve (*****) ✪✪✪✪✪–✪✪✪ *Avenida Tomás Cabreira, Tel. 41 50 01, Fax 41 59 99.* Modern 7-storey luxury hotel facing the beach (private section for hotel guests). Tennis courts, seawater pools, saunas, fitness centre. Disabled access. 220 rooms.

Hotel Apartmento Oriental (****) ✪✪✪ *Avenida Tomás Cabreira, Tel. 41 30 00, Fax 41 34 13.* An attractive, Moorish-style building designed in the style of the casino which stood here in the 1920s. A galleried interior with saunas and a Turkish bath, pleasant gardens with sun terraces and swimming pools looking on to the beach. Disabled access. 85 rooms.

Hotel Bela Vista (****) ✪✪✪ *Avenida Tomás Cabreira, Tel. 24 055, Fax 4153 69* An architectural gem, resembling a church more than a hotel. Built as a summer house in 1916, its interior features beautiful wooden ceilings and staircases plus splendid 19th-century *azulejos*. Request the main house in preference to the annexe. 14 rooms.

Hotel Jupiter (****) ✪✪✪ *Avenida Tomás Cabreira, Tel. 41 50 41, Fax 41 53 19.* A large, modern, 9-storey hotel just off the beach. Swimming pool, shops, and a nightclub. Disabled access. 180 rooms.

Presidente Aparthotel (****) ✪✪✪ *Praia do Vau, Tel. 41 75 07, Fax 41 56 19.* A large tower-block complex offering excellent views over the beach and surrounding country-side. Spacious, well-equipped apartments, swimming pool, small shopping centre. 107 apartments.

Hotel da Rocha (***) ✪–✪✪ *Avenida Tomás Cabreira, Tel. 24 081, Fax 41 59 88.* Good value, simple accommodation in a modern 6-storey block on the seafront. 77 rooms.

Residencial Solar Penguin (**) ✪ *Avenida Tomás Cabreira, Tel. 24 308.* This 75-year-old private house enjoys a magnificent location with the best possible vista of the main beach from its terraces. Charming Old-World atmosphere. 13 rooms.

QUARTEIRA

Hotel Apartmento Atis (***) ✪✪ *Avenida Francisco Sá Carneiro, Tel. 38 97 71, Fax 38 97 74.* Modern, high-rise block overlooking the beach. Small swimming pool. 73 rooms, 40 apartments.

Dom José (***) ✪✪–✪✪✪ *Avenida Infante de Sagres, 145, Tel. 30 27 50; Fax 30 27 55.* Popular beachside hotel catering to package tourists. Pool, disco. Disabled access. 146 rooms.

Zodiaco Hotel (***) ✪✪ *Estrada de Almancil, Tel. 38 95 89, Fax 38 81 15.* Smallish modern hotel set away from the noise and bustle of Quarteira's main strip, but still within easy reach of all facilities. Pleasant rooms with standard equipment, tennis court and swimming pool. 60 rooms.

VALE DO LOBO

Dona Filipa (*****) ✪✪✪✪ *Vale do Lobo, Tel. 39 41 41, Fax 39 42 88.* This Trusthouse Forte hotel is the last word in modern Algarve luxury. Set in 182 hectares (450 acres) with three floodlit tennis courts, it offers beautifully designed bedrooms and public areas, plus a gambling room. Green fees at San Lorenzo golf course included. 147 rooms.

VILAMOURA

Ampalius (****) ✪✪✪ – ✪✪✪✪ *Vilamoura, Tel. 38 80 08; Fax 38 09 11.* This large, modern beachside block is uninspiring from the outside but luxuriously equipped inside. Swimming pool, tennis courts. 357 rooms.

Dom Pedro Golf (****) ✪✪✪ *Vilamoura, Tel. 38 96 50, Fax 31 54 82.* Impressive luxury hotel with large gardens which include three floodlit tennis courts and three pools. Preferential terms for guests at local golf courses. 262 rooms.

Golfe Country Club (Motel do Golfe) (***) ✪✪–✪✪✪ *Vilamoura, Tel. 30 29 75, Fax 38 00 23.* Located on the doorstep of the famous Vilamoura 1 golf course (see page 83), this small hotel is designed with golf lovers in mind but will suit anyone looking for peace and quiet. Set in beautiful, mature grounds with its own par 3 course, plus a superb garden terrace swimming pool. 52 rooms.

Marinotel (*****) ✪✪✪✪ *Vilamoura, Tel. 38 98 58, Fax 38 98 69.* Large, modern, airy state-of-the-art hotel straddling beach and marina. Landscaped grounds with swimming pools plus health club, putting greens, tennis courts, children's park, and excellent restaurants. 389 rooms.

Recommended Restaurants

We enjoyed the food and service in the restaurants listed below; if you find other places that you think are worth recommending, we'd be pleased to hear from you.

To give you an idea of price (for a three-course meal per person, including a half-bottle of house wine) we have used the following symbols:

✪	under 3,500 esc
✪✪	3,500–4,500 esc
✪✪✪	over 4,500 esc

ALBUFEIRA

O Cabaz da Praia (The Beach Basket) ✪✪-✪✪✪ *Praça Miguel Bombarda 7, Tel. 51 21 37.* Enjoy superb French and French-Portuguese food served either on a delightful balcony high above the beach looking out to sea, or in the restaurant's pretty indoor dining room. Excellent, friendly service. Closed Thursday.

A Ruina ✪✪-✪✪✪ *Cais Herculano, Tel. 51 20 94.* Three-tiered *típico* famous for its seafood. Choose among the basic dining room downstairs, rustic restaurant on second floor, and roof-top dining with views over Fishermen's Beach.

Os Arcos ✪✪ *Rua Alves Correira 25, Tel. 51 34 60.* Most Portuguese and budget international favourites are on offer here. The seafood is recommended. Dine outside on the bamboo-covered roof terrace.

Atrium ✪✪ *Rua 5 de Outubro, Tel. 51 57 55.* Quaint, old-fashioned restaurant set in a 100-year-old former theatre. *Arroz marisco* and *cataplana* can be ordered per single person.

Casa da Avó ✪✪✪ *Rua do MFA 97, Tel. 51 44 75.* A well-established, elegant, and stylish dining room dressed in cool pink and white. Interesting and varied menu includes African- and Indian-inspired cuisine, plus a choice of game dishes all year round.

Cave do Vinho do Porto ✪✪ *Rua da Liberdade 23, Tel. 51 32 29.* Romantic and atmospheric brick vaults lined with dusty bottles of Port make this 22-year old institution the ideal place for visitors to get to know the national drink. If you're not sure quite what to choose, ask the friendly proprietor for his advice. The short menu features several Port-flavoured dishes.

O Dias ✪✪ *Praça Miguel Bombarda, Tel. 51 52 46.* Eat out on the charming, tiny terrace of this thatched and *azulejo*-decorated restaurant with its splendid view overlooking the beach. Excellent cheap grills as well as all the usual favourites. Grilled fish is the house speciality. Closed on Thursdays.

Tasca do Viegas ✪✪ *Rua Nova, no telephone bookings.* You can eat or just drink with the locals in this vaulted brick and timber bar-restaurant. Open until late, with a friendly, easy-going atmosphere. Menu features a good selection of shellfish; try also the Steak Portuguêsa.

Três Coroas ✪✪ *Rua Correio Valho 8, Tel. 51 26 40.* This popular, award-winning restaurant offers the usual Portuguese/international menu. It has an attractive large outdoor terrace and a traditional white-washed dining room.

AROUND ALBUFEIRA

La Cigale ✪✪✪ *Praia de Olhos de Água, Tel. 50 16 37.* Excellent seafood in a beautiful rustic, whitewashed beachside restaurant. Perfect for lazy and informal eating by day, La Cigale becomes elegant and romantic by night. Try the *mollusc* *a la cigale*. Other specialities include fondues and the regional favourite, *cataplana*. Closed December-February.

Grill das Amendoeiras ✪✪✪ *Montechoro Hotel, Montechoro, Tel. 58 94 23.* Enjoy the panoramic roof-top view from this stylish blue-and-white dining room. Good international/Portuguese menu with many traditional dishes. Excellent service.

Adega do Zé ✪✪ *2 km (1.2 miles) from Olhos de Agua on road to Albufeira, Tel. 50 16 17.* Rustic-style típico with a large indoor dining area decorated throughout with bric-a-brac. Grills are the speciality of the house, with a huge choice of fish on the menu. Also features regular folklore shows.

Pinhal do António ✪✪ *Roja Pé, Açoteias Road (opposite Sheraton Algarve, Pine Cliffs Hotel), Tel. 503 87.* Unassuming café-restaurant with a small roadside terrace outside and a large traditional dining room inside. Good, straightforward Portuguese cooking. Fish and shellfish are the specialities of the house.

Três Palmeiras ✪✪ *Areias de São João, coast road to Albufeira, Tel. 51 54 23.* This smart indoor restaurant is popular with both locals and tourists alike. Choose from a variety of daily specials, with fish always prominent on the menu. Closed Sunday.

ALMANSIL

Pequeno Mundo ✪✪✪ *Almansil, just off Quarteira Road, Tel. 39 98 66.* In a charming setting of renovated cottages, gourmet-standard international cuisine is prepared by an English proprietor. Don't miss out on the delicious fig and almond frangipane tart. Closed Monday.

FARO

Cidale Velha ✪✪✪ *Rua Domingos Guieiro 19 (Old Town), Tel. 27 145.* A lovely, intimate, romantic restaurant set in the old quarter of Faro. Smallish Portuguese/international menu—try the fried crab cakes and the house speciality, *lombinho de porco* house-style (pork fillet stuffed with dates and walnuts). Closed Sunday.

Green Steak House ✪✪–✪✪✪ *Rua Pé da Cruz, Tel. 82 13 03.* Small but smart restaurant. House specialities are *cataplana* and steaks. Reservations necessary. Closed Sunday.

Dois Irmãos ✪✪ *Largo do Terreiro do Bispo 18, Tel. 23 337.* The Two Brothers restaurant has been a Faro fish legend since as long ago as 1925. A large establishment with an extensive seafood menu, including nine types of *cataplana* alone. Lots of regional specials for you to choose from.

Café Chelsea ✪–✪✪ *Rua de Francisco Gomes 28, Tel. 28 459.* The bright, white, modern downstairs room here is perfect for a daytime snack, while the elegant blue-and-white upstairs fits the bill for eating out on more formal occasions. Wide-ranging menu includes dishes from pizzas to shellfish specials.

LAGOS

O Alpendre ✪✪✪ *Rua Barbosa Viana, Tel. 76 27 05.* You can sample a broad range of Portuguese/international cuisine, as well as regional dishes and fish specialities in the traditional setting of this well-respected establishment.

Dom Sebastião ✪✪✪ *Rua 25 de Abril 20–22, Tel. 76 27 95.* Live seafood is the speciality at this very popular, attractive rustic-style restaurant. Closed Sunday October-May.

Dom Henrique ✪✪ *Rua 25 de Abril 75, Tel. 76 35 63.* Classic Portuguese/international cuisine is served in a formal, traditional dining room. Recommended in particular for its excellent seafood dishes.

O Galeão ✪ *Rua da Lanranjeira 1, Tel. 76 39 09.* The owner-chef and his Swiss-trained team have made this small, traditional restaurant one of Lagos's most popular eating places. Fondue, *cataplana* or sole Algarvian are the house specialities. Closed Sunday.

Piri-Piri ✪ *Rua Alfonso d'Almedia, Tel. 63 803.* Large menu, featuring local shellfish dishes, and some interesting, if unusual, meat-based recipes (including turkey with raisins). All served up in fairly standard but pleasant surroundings.

Jotta 13 ✪–✪✪ *Rua 25 de Abril 58, Tel. 76 23 19.* Bright, basic decor and furnishings and a standard Portuguese/international menu; Jotta 13 is better known for its quality and value than atmosphere and trimmings.

Dos Reis ✪ *Rua António Barbosa Viana 21, Tel. 62 900.* This brightly-lit, informal establishment is well-recommended in Lagos circles for its classic Portuguese/international cuisine.

AROUND LAGOS

O Caseiro ✪–✪✪ *Arão (on main road from EN 125), Tel. 79 91 69.* Off the beaten track, set in the heart of unspoiled countryside, O Caseiro caters for locals, at locals' prices, but also welcomes tourists. Simple fish and shellfish menu with several fish and meat specials. The dining room is large, but red gingham trimmings give it a more homely feel.

Villalisa ✪ *Mexilheira Grande, on right-hand side main road (off EN 125), no telephone bookings.* There's no sign outside to help you, so look for the low house with the bright blue-and-yellow window panels (or just ask in the village). Inside there are no frills either. You may get a choice or you may just be served dish of the day. Recommended by everyone who knows it.

MONCHIQUE-FOIA

Rampa ✪–✪✪ *Monchique-Foia Road, Tel. 92 620.* One of several good roadside restaurants with terraces enjoying panoramic views, Rampa is small and friendly. Go for the *frango piri-piri*, which comes in mountainous portions to echo the view, or snack on grilled quail. Eel is also a house speciality.

PORTIMÃO

A Lanterna ✪✪ *Portimão Bridge (Ferragudo side), Tel. 23 948.* Long-established and well-known with a reputation for high quality, A Lanterna offers elegant dining in small, traditionally furnished rooms. Specials include smoked fish and some interesting desserts. Closed Sunday.

Avózinha ✪✪ *Rua do Capote 7, Tel. 22 922.* "Grandma's" has been serving award-winning fish and shellfish for over 20 years in Portimão. *Cataplanas* are a speciality.

Bonjour Goodnight ✪✪ *Rua Serpa Pinto 22 (by the bridge), Tel. 22 516.* Gaudy neon signs and brimming aquariums give a lively, bustling feel to this small restaurant. Specialists in *cataplana,* and claiming the cheapest shellfish on the Algarve. Open late.

O Buque ✪✪ *Portimão Bridge (Ferragudo side), Tel. 24 678.* Attractive dining room with traditional furniture, nautical nicknacks, and colourful tartan table-cloths. Interesting Portuguese/international menu with several daily specials available.

Tipoia ✪✪ *Rua da Senhora da Tocha 10, Tel. 26 118.* Tucked away in a back street, this small, rusticized, 10-year-old restaurant offers the town's most varied menu, including dishes such as shrimp curry, baked kid, and suckling pig. Mozambique influences. Don't miss the house dessert. Closed Wednesday.

Casa Bica ✪ *The Quayside, no telephone bookings.* It doesn't have to be at long-established Casa Bica, as the ramshackle dockside diners are all much the same, but it is obligatory to eat sardines by the quay at Portimão. Casa Bica also offer a selection of other grilled fish.

PRAIA DA ROCHA

A Balança ✪✪ *Avenida Tomás Cabreira.* Go alfresco on the splendid large terrace with sea view, rather than dine in the restaurant's bland, modern interior. Portuguese/international cuisine.

Falésia ✪✪ *Avenida Tomás Cabreira, Tel. 23 524.* Elegant, formal dining in an historic old mansion. One dining room looks onto the beach, another has arches and decoration in the Moorish-style. Portuguese/international cuisine.

Safari ✪✪ *Rua António Feu (between Avenida Tomás Cabreira and the beach), Tel. 41 55 40.* A slice of Portuguese colonial Africa, with stuffed animal's heads on the wall, and dishes like Chicken Curry and Lamb Angolan style on an otherwise Portuguese/international menu. Friendly management from Angola.

Titanic ✪✪ *Ediffício Columbia, Rua Eng Francisco Bivar, Tel. 22 371.* Formal and flouncy decor, with an open kitchen, serving good quality international cuisine.

Fortaleza de Santa Caterina ✪ *Avenida Tomás Cabreira, Tel. 22 066.* Set in the courtyard of the 16th-century castle, this simple restaurant specializes in fish. Large picture windows make this a perfect place to dine as you watch the sun go down.

The Penguin Terrace ✪ *Avenida Tomás Cabreira (next to Residencial Solar Penguin), Tel. 24 308.* Halfway down the steps to the beach, this, pretty terrace restaurant with its friendly staff is perfect for a beachside snack and a beautiful location for an informal evening meal. Try the chicken *piri-piri* and their excellent salads.

AROUND PRAIA DA ROCHA

Ao Mar ✪✪ *Rua dos Castelos, Praia do Vau, Tel. 41 39 83.* An attractive, modern, blue-and-white chalet-style building right on the beach with a bright, stylish interior and a lovely terrace. Portuguese/international cuisine with changing specials. (Within walking distance of the centre of Praia da Rocha.)

Alvila ✪✪✪ *Praia da Rocha-Alvor Road (1km/0.6 miles from Alvor), Tel. 45 87 75.* A modern restaurant, quite small but at its Moorish best on the Tuesday *fado* night, which always proves popular with visitors. Flambés are a speciality of the house.

QUARTEIRA

Os Pescadores ✪✪ *Largo Cortés Real (opposite fish market), Tel. 31 47 55.* Small, modern restaurant with nautical, cork decor. Good value fish and meat dishes.

O Buzio ✪–✪✪ *just off fish market, Tel. 31 57 25.* Cheap and cheerful establishment, with red-and-white gingham tablecloths and blue-and-white *azulejos.* Excellent value fish and shellfish. Also features regular live entertainment.

SAGRES

Restaurante Cabo de São Vicente ✪✪–✪✪✪ *Fortaleza do Beliche (5km/3 miles east of Sagres), Tel. 64 124.* This charming, formal, pousada restaurant (the fortaleza is annexed to the pousada at Sagres) is set in the historic remains of a 17th-century fortress, serving traditional, regional food.

VILAMOURA

The Mayflower ✪✪–✪✪✪ *The Marina, Vilamoura, Tel. 31 46 90.* Eat out on the pretty terrace, perfect for alfresco dining. Inside, the restaurant is decorated with rich wood and marble. The menu is good value, and offers a varied choice of dishes.

ABOUT BERLITZ

In 1878 Professor Maximilian Berlitz had a revolutionary idea about making language learning accessible and enjoyable. One hundred and twenty years later these same principles are still successfully at work.

For language instruction, translation and interpretation services, cross-cultural training, study abroad programs, and an array of publishing products and additional services, visit any one of our more than 350 Berlitz Centers in over 40 countries.

Please consult your local telephone directory for the Berlitz Center nearest you or visit our web site at http://www.berlitz.com.

BERLITZ
Fremdsprachen

Helping the World Communicate